Over the hills and far away

# HARFORD LOGAN

Harford Logan, from County Down in Northern Ireland, has been winning and judging sheepdog trials for over fifty years. He has won seven National Championships, six for Ireland and one for Scotland, represented Ireland at international level at least twenty-two times, Scotland on three occasions and been in the Supreme Championship, the top fifteen handlers in the country, on seven occasions over the years. He has competed on three occasions on the BBC programme *One Man and His Dog*, winning the Brace Competition in 1988. He is also one of the world's most experienced sheepdog trial judges and has regularly been invited to judge trials in America, Canada and across Europe. Harford is a Director of the International Sheepdog Society and continues to lobby for the very highest standards of sheepdog breeding and handling and for the integrity of the sheepdog trial itself.

# Over the hills and far
## away

*The escapades and winning ways of*
*Harford Logan and his border collies*

Harford Logan
Joanne McHardy

**Spirita
Books**

Copyright © Harford Logan & Joanne McHardy 2006
Illustrations in text © Holly Bennet 2006
First published in 2006 by Spirita Books
P O Box 2222, Pulborough, RH20 6AA

Revised Second Edition 2014

Book trade distribution by Lightning Source/Spirita Books

British Library Cataloguing in Publication Data
A catalogue record for this book is available from the British Library.

ISBN 978-0-9552762-1-7

Typeset by Amolibros, Milverton, Somerset
This book production has been managed by Amolibros
Printed and bound by Lightning Source

# Table of Contents

*Harford and Star win the Scottish National, Glamis Castle 1981.*

# Introduction by E B Raley

My serious interest in sheepdogs dates back to the late seventies at a time when our own farming and ranching operation in Texas included winter grazing of wheat fields with both sheep and stocker cattle. Both of my boys were keen on using horses to manage the cattle, but it was Berry, the eldest, who became interested in Border Collies and soon learned to train and use them in our own operations. With my wife's encouragement, this became an opportunity to justify involvement in the sport of sheepdog trialling. At that time there were no good trained dogs in this area of Texas and I was soon convinced that dogs imported from Britain were needed for the job. That was the way to go! Berry and I planned a trip to trials in Britain, which would include the Scottish National at Glamis. Each day of the trial we carefully observed handlers whose names were a source of expectation as to the National Champion. Some of them that come to mind were Peter Hetherington, Johnny Templeton, Willy Welsh, Jock Welsh, John Angus McCloud, and a lesser known (to us) transplanted Irishman, Harford Logan. We were very novice in our ability to judge quality runs but we knew we were watching something very special when the crowd sat in hushed silence on that morning when Harford Logan and Star were on the field. When the pen gate closed it was evident that a great pair of competitors had just made their mark – Harford & Star. Somehow, Harford began to help me with purchases in Scotland of sheepdogs for import to US. Sage advice from him kept me from making bad deals and helped me secure good dogs for my own use. I have always been impressed by the respect and friendship which Harford enjoys wherever he is. From him I have not only learned to enjoy humour as only the Irish can provide, I have also been humbled by his own genuine interest in others and generosity of spirit. I have no idea how many dog deals he and I have shared, but I must say that his knowledge and recommendations have had me in the winner's circle many times. Few men have I seen who are as admired and welcomed in the sheepdog world as this man. Friends gather to his side and renew friendships everywhere he goes. I commend this book to those who want to learn about sheepdogs, sheep farming and enjoy a full dose of Irish humour at the side of none other than the master – Harford Logan.

# Foreword

As I look back on a lifetime of working with and judging some world class border collies I have begun to reflect on just how much I have learnt from those dogs and from the many countrymen and shepherds I have met over the years. Whilst many things have moved on in the world of shepherding and sheepdog trialling, to my mind the fundamental keys to success remain the same. Many people see the relationship between the dog and its handler as most important, likening the authority of the handler to that of a pack leader asserting his power. But for a shepherd it's more complicated than that and it would be arrogant to assume that as a handler, we should try to control completely the relationship between the dog and the sheep – or assume a dog so intelligent will be better under our command at all times. For me, the secret to success is to have a dog that can make friends with and command the respect of the sheep. It doesn't bother me too much if a dog doesn't get on too well with people (unless of course it is dangerous). Their ability to build a relationship with the sheep is what is most important, and is what sets a champion dog aside from the rest. Some experienced working dogs need to feel they are in control of the relationship with the sheep if you are to get the best from them. It's a very complex relationship and every dog is different. But it is this triangular relationship between handler, dog and sheep that sets a working border collie apart from one that is simply a companion. Whilst authority on behalf of the handler is important with regards to a pet dog, with a working dog it is all about partnership and mutual respect. And respect is certainly something I have in abundance for the working sheepdog. A dog that has been bred to do the job of ten shepherds but with intelligence, courage and style. A dog that is always willing to give of their all, and then, when we've taken them to show off their brilliance at sheepdog trials, sits back modestly while we pick up the silver.

In this book, I've tried not to write a purely technical handbook on sheepdogs and trials – a lot of folk have done that far too well already. I do though explain what I have found to be a sound way to build a strong handler, sheepdog partnership, and what it takes to win a trial.

And of course, when you've been farming with sheepdogs and judging for as long as I have you tend to have a few stories to swap with those around you – stories about the country characters we teased as boys, the escapades of our younger sporting days and, in more serious moments, the land we farmed and the stock we reared. I've named a few folk and a lot of places, but not everyone and everywhere that deserves a mention. Bear with me if in the enthusiasm of telling the story I've got some of the details wrong.

At the very least, I hope the following pages provide some entertainment. If they give you some tips and tactics you can use to improve the way you work with your dog, then even better.

*Banbridge on market day – Photograph courtesy of Dennis Quayle*

# EARLY DAYS

## Shanaghan Farm

My journey began in a place called Shanaghan in Katesbridge, County Down. My grandfather could count that I was the eighth generation of the Logan family living on Shanaghan Farm – there could actually have been more but that was as far back as he could count. All four of my children were also born there, so that makes it at least nine generations of us in that small corner of Ireland.

The farm house sat fairly high up in the rolling hills typical of the countryside, at the end of a long winding lane of about a mile, off which two neighbours' farms were found. Katesbridge boasted a two-roomed school, two mills, one corn, the other flax, a blacksmith shop, and in time a phone box on the cross roads. Besides the bridge over the River Bann which gave the village its name, there was not a lot more, but for a long time it was the centre of my universe.

Many an idle moment was spent around the corn mill's swooshing water wheel or checking out the horses being shod at the blacksmith's shop. The corn mill bruised oats for cattle, except on a Tuesday, when we'd call in after school to get a handful of fresh oaten meal which was being ground for porridge or oaten bread. On our school holidays we were sometimes sent to help at the flax mill which was driven by steam, its tall chimney standing proud against the landscape.

The average farm at that time in County Down was around

1

twenty-five acres. A family would have been reared on a farm that size. Shanaghan was a mixed arable, livestock farm and at fifty acres, with maybe the same again rented from a neighbour, was a reasonably large farm for the time.

We had six milking cows whose calves, together with others bought in, were reared for meat. The cows were hand-milked and the surplus milk made into butter which the local people in the village would buy from my mother once a week, the residue skimmed milk then being fed to the pigs. It would take around fifty pounds of butter a week to supply those who came to our farm, and this was part of the farm income. We kept a flock of pedigree Border Leicester sheep as well as some Scotch Blackface. There were also twenty breeding sows and five hundred free range poultry. Pigs and hens were a good source of income on a small farm at that time. Besides the livestock, we grew about ten acres of potatoes and twenty acres of oats. We threshed the hay and sold the seed to a merchant. A farm labourer was kept full time, and at springtime, harvest time and in winter, when we were potato sorting, there would have been at least one extra man. Work was all manual at that time.

My father did not have trial sheepdogs, but he always kept useful farm dogs. As a boy I was very attached to these border collies, and one especially, Shep, who let me ride on his back. When I started school I had a choice of two-mile walks to get there. One was down our lane to the main road and the other was what we called the 'back lane', going down by Kernaghan's farm, taking me out on to a different road. About once or twice a week, depending on where I had been with my friends, I would come home by the back road. Somehow though, Shep always seemed to sense where I'd be and no matter which lane I chose, he'd be there to meet me half way. He just seemed to have great instinct and loved children.

My father was also a keen horse man, breeding and showing Clydesdales. Most years we would have a Clydesdale in foal and there was always great excitement to see what the new foal would be like – whether it was a potential winner or not. He also kept a half-bred horse which was used to go into town, about eight miles away, as it was fast on the road. I heard him say that when he was in his teens he always ploughed with a Clydesdale and a half bred horse. There were a lot of hunt packs in County Down and the County Down Stag Hounds who were close by hunted twice a week. If my father was ploughing in the winter time and the stag-hounds came through, he would tie the Clydesdale horse to the fence, take the harness off the half-bred horse and get on its back to follow the hunt to the finish. He would then come back to the field, re-harness the half-bred and plough for the rest of the day. At that time hunting was great excitement in the country. The further the hunt went the bigger the crowd that followed.

Like my father, I had a keen interest in showing sheep and horses from a very early age. As a boy on Saturdays in the winter, I would bring a foal into the yard and teach it to lead. When no one was around I would wash its legs and get some sawdust as if I was getting it ready for showing. I would do the same with any Border Leicester lamb which I thought could be a champion. I would sneak the sheep shears out of the barn and dress it up as if I was getting it ready for a show. As far as I was concerned I had always picked the winner.

But it was the sheepdogs that were my real heroes. When my class was asked by the school master to draw what we would like to be when we grew up, my friends sketched themselves in the kind of jobs which were familiar to them during those war years – doctors, school teachers, ambulance drivers. My head was somewhere else entirely. I drew a picture of me walking over a hill with the aid of a well-made crook, a fine flock of sheep ahead and the best dog in the country at my side. 'Nice drawing,' says Master Curry, 'but where's your ambition, boy!' giving me a sharp clip round the ear. Maybe he didn't appreciate that in that simple drawing I had included a champion sheepdog. Or maybe he just couldn't see how anybody could be content to devote a lifetime to shepherding. He probably remained unimpressed when in a few years' time that drawing was transformed into a picture of me and my dogs on the front of the *Belfast Telegraph* after I was a surprise winner of a major sheepdog trial. But then everyone has a different idea of success and what it takes to be happy. Mine's always been fairly straightforward and even now, given the chance to go back to that classroom, I wouldn't change a thing in that drawing.

## Cap – The First Sheepdog I Trained

The first sheepdog I could call my own was Cap, a small black and tan collie, his mother a working farm bitch, her ancestry unknown, but his sire, also Cap, a naturally talented dog who had won many trials for a Mr Hugh Holmes. Mr Holmes was a Baptist pastor who had bought the dog as a puppy in the North of England. My Cap was not as stylish as his sire but a very clever dog. Some of the things he could do were almost unbelievable.

Cap did not need many commands. We just talked to him like any other person. About fifteen minutes before milking, I would say, 'Go and get the cows, Cap,' and by the time the byre was ready for milking, Cap had the cows at the gate. The cows would have had the run of four or five fields and he would have had to drive them in a number of different directions before arriving home with them, and most often having to bring them through the sheep grazing in the fields as well. When told to bring the sheep, he would bring the sheep through the cattle.

One of the very first commands I set out to teach Cap was the 'Shed' – that's separating one or more of the flock away from the others on command – on account of a breakout of my mother's free range roosters. Cap was commandeered to help catch these escapees which were by now all mixed up with the hens, running amok around the yard and fields. He had quickly figured out that the rooster made a different noise from the hens and so when given the command, he would pounce gently and comically on the rooster holding it down with his two front paws. Cap remembered that 'get the rooster' command all his life. No matter where he was, he would look around in earnest for the rooster when I asked him to get it for me.

He was also a useful gun dog for both rabbits or pheasants, always seeming to know where they were. He would stand stock still and seem to give me a wink to let me know there was some game in hiding. If Cap told me they were there, I could always be sure he was right.

Most of all, he was invaluable on the road taking sheep and cattle to market as he would slip through fences and stand in lane-ways. He knew exactly the right place to be. If there wasn't any stock to come home from market, he would jump on to my back on the bicycle with his two paws over my shoulders. It did not matter how fast I went round corners, he held on. He would even ride on our driving and cross country pony which stayed around the farmyard. On a cold day it was not unusual to see Cap lying on the pony's back, possibly for the warmth of his body.

Cap was certainly not a robot. He seemed to think about

5

the commands he was given and who was giving them. On one occasion, after taking stock to the local market in Rathfriland, a neighbouring farmer had bought some blackface ewe lambs and asked me if he could have the lend of Cap to help him get them home. I started them all off out of town and gave the farmer instructions on the commands Cap knew. After some time Cap arrived home in the yard with the lambs, not convinced the neighbouring farmer should be taking them anywhere else. Only once he was reassured that we were happy about the transaction did he set about transferring them to our neighbour's farm.

Not that Cap was the only clever dog. Folk were always telling stories about the antics of their own border collies. One in particular, a chap who was famous for telling tall stories, was forever boasting about how well his dog managed the stock, almost without any commands at all, bringing the cows in each morning and evening without him having to tell him it was time. But that wasn't all. He said there was one day when the dog didn't appear with the cows as usual and it was getting later and later. He began to wonder what the heck was going on. He knew the cows would be roaring if they weren't soon milked. Just as he was about to stalk off to the fields himself, he heard the cows coming up the lane, and sure enough in a few minutes his dog, Jim, had them all in the yard. The cows filed into the byre one by one and ambled to their usual stalls. He claimed he was busy getting on with his milking, his temper cooled by now, when in trots Jim to the byre and, bold as brass, swishes his tail about in a pail of milk. He gave out a roar and chased the dog out of his sight, disgusted that it seemed to have taken leave of its senses. But the dog wasn't to be intimidated. In a few minutes in he walks calm as you like with a new born calf sucking his tail. He'd apparently taken time in the fields to supervise the birth of the calf and, seeing that the mother wasn't feeding it, he'd brought it to the yard for some attention. So if that was true, that was one clever dog.

## Farming the Hard Way

There was a lot of manual work on the farm at this time. We'd prepare and fertilise our ground, then sow and reap our crops all with fairly basic equipment by today's standards. Sometimes we'd have the power of our horses, usually Clydesdales, to help. At other times, such as when we were sowing corn or spraying potatoes, we were on our own. And across the countryside, we'd all be absolutely reliant on each other. We'd not only lend our efforts to the task in hand, we'd also pool our equipment and horses to lighten the load. There were unwritten rules of fairness when it came to farming. Without too much debate, or any need for formal contracts, you always knew when you owed a neighbour a favour, or when you could call one in. Looking back, it was a time of hard, physical labour, not all of it very healthy or pleasant, but it was also a time of great camaraderie – and that made all the difference.

But it wasn't sweet and easy all of the time. Something that wasn't much liked was a situation where two farmers just weren't getting on or maybe not even speaking to each other as a result of some feud or other. These feuds were more often than not over something of no consequence but some old farmers could brood for eternity if they were allowed. As young men we tended to see this as an opportunity for a bit of sport. One trick was to take the cart from one farm and swap it with the cart from the other with the result that the two farmers would have to get in touch to make arrangements to get their carts back from one another.

One of the most labour intensive winter jobs was putting out the farmyard manure. Now you'd think this would be a fairly simple job, but my father was very particular about these things. The cart had to be filled from the midden and then drawn to the fields and put out in piles on stubble ground to be ploughed in for potatoes. The challenge would be to put it out of the cart in straight lines, each pile the same distance apart. Whether you looked up or across the field, all piles had to be in perfectly straight lines and then spread over the field to give even coverage.

And then there was the potato planting. Potatoes were an important crop, grown as food for the stock and family as well as being a source of income for the farm. There was always a large acreage devoted to growing them and if potato stores were not available on the farm, the potatoes were put in pits in a field. Many a winter's day I sat on my knees at the edge of the pit and selecting small potatoes for seed, bigger ones for market and setting aside any with a blemish for stock feeding. Farmyard manure was spread in the bottom of the drill and the potatoes planted on top before the drills were covered. I heard my grandfather say that in the year of the Irish potato famine, so few potatoes were sound that the pit was not needed. They could all be stored in just one barrel which was guarded for next year's seed. None could be eaten. Oaten meal from

Katesbridge Mill was what kept the people alive. There was a meeting point where the starving and homeless would gather to be given oaten meal gruel to keep them going.

Some of the hardest manual work was spraying potatoes with blue stone and washing ashes dissolved in water. If this remedy had been available earlier, there would not have been a potato famine as it prevented blight which was the cause of the famine. It was heavy work carrying a knapsack sprayer through the long potato foliage. The spray was made up in barrels at the end of the drills and the water drawn from rivers or wells with the horse and cart. If the field was steep you had to measure your pace going up and downhill to make sure the drills got the same amount of spray. The relief getting to the end of one drill was short-lived as the copper sprayers were then filled for the next drill and off you had to go again.

There was always considered to be a great deal of skill involved in sowing corn with the corn fiddle. As with the potato sprayer, you had to keep the same speed going up and down the field, taking care that each cast was about three yards apart. If this was not done the corn would grow in stripes and be visible from a long distance – the butt of jokes by the neighbouring farmers.

But it was threshing that was one of the biggest operations of the farming year. In late summer, oats and hay had to be drawn out of the stacks in the stackyard and stored in the barn in readiness to be fed into the threshing machine. The horses went round the horse-walk outside the barn to drive the threshing machine, often with me riding on the thresher shaft as they circled round. We could hardly see each other for dust inside the barn, especially when threshing hay. After threshing, the hay and straw was drawn back to the stackyard and built in stacks for winter-feed while the oat and grass seed was put through hand-turned fans in the barn to be cleaned ready for the seed merchants. Farmers took a sample of seed to the merchants in

Banbridge on market day, a Monday, and the merchant would give them a price according to quality.

After the horse-driven era, the next advance was the advent of more efficient engine-driven threshing machines which travelled from farm to farm. The engines of these mills started running on petrol and then switched over to paraffin oil – or TVO (tractor vaporising oil) as we called it. Matt Ferguson owned the first threshing machine I remember seeing, but he didn't own a tractor. As a result we would have to take two horses to the farm where he was working if we wanted him to thresh for us. One was to collect the mill and the other to collect the engine. His next customer would have the same routine, arriving at our farm with their two horses. Until everyone's threshing was done we'd all follow Matt's threshing machine around the country helping out on our neighbour's farms, as they'd helped out on ours.

Matt was quite a character always telling stories. He once told of a time when he went up to a farm in the Mourne Mountain country. There was threshing for a week and little help at this farm as they did not help anyone else. Not wanting to go, he'd told the farmer he would only go on one condition, that he would get beef for dinner every day. The first day he was presented with beef, turnip and potatoes. On the second day the farmer's wife rationed the beef. On the remaining three days she just served up turnip and potatoes.

At the end of the week Matt said to the lady of the house, 'The deal I made was beef every day. I only got it two days and on the second day very little.'

'If you had got any more beef the cattle would have been roaring in you,' she cracked back.

'By God it wouldn't have been for the want of turnips,' was his reply.

Winter on the farm consisted of feeding stock, cleaning out houses, ploughing and helping neighbours to thresh, which didn't leave much time for other farm work.

Water had to be pumped by hand from the well in the yard for the animals to drink. They seemed to drink twice as much when pumping by hand as they do now. Pigs had water barrels in their pens which were kept filled and there were automatic drinking bowls fitted to the barrels. Any available time was spent drawing out farmyard manure with the spare horse. The remaining horses were kept ploughing most of the wintertime when the weather was favourable.

When I was a boy I loved to listen to my grandfather telling me stories and especially to hear the banter between the old characters. A lot of these old boys prided themselves on their horsemanship and especially how that manifested itself in the straightness of their potato drills. Heaven forbid if they were caught making a drill with a bit of bend in it. On one particular occasion I overheard the banter between a postman who kept a lurcher, a cross between a greyhound and a collie, and a local farmer who very much prided himself on the straightness of his drills. There were quite a few lurchers around at that time as they were used to catch rabbits and hares through the country. The farmer was making little of this postman's lurcher. He wasn't too impressed with its breeding and didn't think it was likely to catch too many hares.

'Aye,' says the postman, having listened to this abuse for a long while. 'My old lurcher does lose the odd hare right enough, he doesn't just catch them all. In fact the other day when I was going round delivering the mail he put a hare up but lost him going round the third bend on your drills.'

# A World of Horses

A job which my father would enjoy and reserve entirely for himself was breaking in a Clib, the name used for a young horse one and a half years old. As they matured they took their place on the team of four horses so there was always a four- or five-year-old for sale each year. A horse dealer called James McAvoy mostly bought these and many of them went to London to pull drays.

When young horses started to work it was important to be very careful with their shoulders as their skin could be very easily scalded or broken. A common remedy for hardening the skin after a short spell of work was to bring out the chamber pot and pour urine over their shoulders.

Horse ploughmen took great pride in their work and a good ploughman could plough an Irish acre in a day – a much bigger area than statute measure. Ploughmen in Scotland had a secret society and had a word they used to identify each other called 'The Horseman's Word'. Strictly speaking, one had to be a member of this society to know the Horseman's Word, but someone shared the secret with me. If you look hard enough back over this paragraph you will find the secret word too.

There was always the odd careless ploughman though and one such ploughman was a man in our area. He took life easy, didn't start too early and his horses were not too well fed with the result that they were unable to do a full day's work – something that suited him fine. One day he was ploughing hard grassy ground, or a ley rig as it was called, and his language was not good. The Minister came up the road on the bicycle and unknown to John was standing behind the hedge. 'Could you not do your work without this terrible language, John?'

'Maybe in stubble ground but not in ley, Your Reverence,' was the reply.

The horses at Shanaghan were always fed four times daily whether they were working or not. In total they would not get more than other farm horses but they were fed on the principle of little and often and seemed to do well with this method of feeding.

On one occasion on a Saturday morning, when I was around twelve years old, I was sent to Dan Morgan's, the village farrier, to get a mare shod. This mare, Dolly, was used at ploughing matches but was also very stylish and very high tempered. She was often shown in the 'Style and Appearance Class', a class which she and her sister had won as a team.

The Blacksmith Shop was on the edge of the River Bann and the blacksmith's residence was on the edge of the river as well. On the occasion of high floods both the shop and the dwelling were often flooded. Dan the blacksmith told the story of his grandfather who one Sunday morning, thinking he heard the chapel bell ringing and that he was late for mass, jumped out of bed only to find he was in water to his knees. There had been heavy rain during the night and unknown to him the river had flooded. What he thought was the chapel bell was actually the chamber pot floating and knocking against the iron bedstead.

Anyway, on this morning when I arrived at the blacksmith shop there were a number of horses in the queue which meant I had to wait outside with a cold and restless Dolly for quite a while until our turn came. After having her shod and getting back out on to the road, she started to play up and boss me around as she well could at that time. She was squealing and rearing up on her hind legs, with the danger of her coming down on me with her front feet. Says I, 'My girl if I could get you over to that wall I could climb on your back and you wouldn't tramp on me.' This I managed to do but the relief was short-lived. We'd only managed to get up the road a short distance when lo and behold, being wartime, I met a convoy of army tanks and off she bolted. I could do nothing but hold on as we galloped faster and faster round bend after bend, dodging what turned out to be a mile-long convoy of big old, lumbering tanks. They seemed too big for the wee narrow, winding country roads and there was very little space for Dolly in full flight.

A family of Belfast people evacuated during the war who were taking a slow amble up Shanaghan Lane threw themselves into the hedge as Dolly and I thundered on. But there were a few more obstacles to negotiate on the way, one in particular being our neighbour's farmyard. As usual it was full of hens,

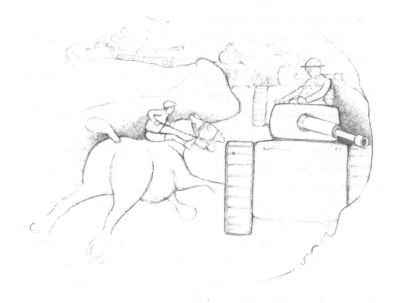

but not for long. I was still wearing a few of them when Dolly eventually came to a halt at her stable door. Before I could jump off Dolly's back, my father appeared in the farmyard.

'In future,' he says, in his most sombre voice, 'be a bit more careful when you get a horse shod.'

Which in truth was just what I was trying to do.

## Markets & Fairs

**M**uch of the timing of the work on the farm centred around the local market days in Banbridge, Rathfriland and Dromore. There were also the monthly fairs which were big social, as well as business, occasions.

Banbridge was a busy town and a good market town, the fair day being the last Monday of each month. There were also three large horse fairs there every year, on the twelfth of January, the ninth of June and the twenty-sixth of August. Horses and dealers came from far and wide and the town was full of people.

These days were the highlights of the year. Besides the hundreds of horses and donkeys lining the streets, there would be other attractions such as side shows, guys lying on beds of nails and men walking through hot coals – and the many pick-pockets that go with crowds of that sort. Many young people met their partners on a fair day when the towns would be full of people.

In those days the stock, cattle and sheep were driven to market on foot and it could often be the case that in the winter months villages and towns would be cut off for weeks as the result of heavy snowfalls. One such heavy fall of snow happened on market day one twelfth of January, an event recalled by older generations. The horses and people were stranded in the town and many of the horses died of starvation before the roads were eventually opened manually by shovels.

If we were taking sheep to market I would set off with Cap to a field near town the night before, whereas with cattle we would start off in the darkness very early on the same day. Cap was well used to the road to town and, without needing to be told, was always into the gaps and laneways to head the animals in the right direction. Until daytime came I would go in front on the bicycle with a torch to warn oncoming traffic which at that time was only the occasional bus. During wartime and for a time afterwards few people had cars and those who had were doctors or people who owned them out of necessity. As petrol was rationed, even those who had them rarely used them.

Around the markets were a number of restaurants, called Eating Houses by the farming community, and actually more or less tea-rooms. A story is told of a cattle dealer from the Bangor area that bought a lot of cattle at the fairs and who was well-known for his appetite, being a big man of almost thirty stone. Apparently he was well used to settling down to a large meal when he had finished his dealings in the fair. On one occasion the portion control was apparently not to his liking. When the waitress had set down his food along with, in his view, a none-too generous portion of honey in a dish his comment was, 'I see, Ma'am, that you keep a bee.'

Sometimes my father went by train or bus to the market while, a farm worker we had, Paddy McPolin, and I would take the cattle to market on foot. I remember one bullock especially. My father at one time bought a Jersey cow in calf. We had hoped for a heifer, but unfortunately it was a bull calf by an Ayrshire bull. This cross Jersey/Ayrshire was just worthless for beef but it was reared with the other calves. When it was about three years old we tried to fatten it. But it was impossible. So when we had some fat cattle going to Rathfriland Market, we decided to take this bullock, Old Brindle we called him, thinking someone would buy him for small money as he was eating as much as a good quality beast.

We sold the fat cattle and there were a lot of people looking at Old Brindle but no one bid for him. Father having a pride in good stock did not stay close-by as he did not want anyone to know it was his. He told me if anyone bid money to give him to them.

It came to late afternoon and most of the stock on the town street was sold but not Old Brindle. Stock was herded around shop doors and town squares. The shops did not mind as it brought in plenty of trade, the old saying, 'Where there's muck there's money'. So at the end of the day I headed home with Old Brindle. It was just a matter of following him because he remembered his road.

Old Brindle was three times in Rathfriland and Father always left me to do the selling while he stayed well away and talked to other farmers. Each type of stock had its own place in town. My father would spend most of his time at the horse section, or the milk cows.

After all this time going to Rathfriland someone told Father if he took him to Banbridge Fair a cattle dealer from Portadown who attended Banbridge and bought poor quality cattle might be interested. So the following Banbridge Fair we took a few other beasts to sell, one being an in-calf cow. In-calf cows were sold under the bridge in Banbridge and there were always quite a few characters amongst the cow dealers. They were able with the tongue and could give a good answer. One such was Joe Russell who was a well respected dealer. At one time he'd sold a cow at small money. After the buyer paid for the cow he said to Joe, 'Mr Russell, I like the cow and you didn't charge me a big price. There will probably be some wee thing wrong about her, but it will not make any difference now.'

'Well,' Joe says, 'she has just got one wee fault. She hasn't got very much milk, but if she had, she's the girl would give it to you.'

It was a longer journey to Banbridge Fair – about eight miles, Rathfriland being around six – and about two miles out of town there was a water pump on the side of the road with a cloth cap sat on top. It was a clear summer morning and as usual I was on the bicycle up front with my father walking behind with the stock. I went over and lifted the cap off the pump and put it on my head. My father, thinking I was helping myself to someone else's cap says, 'Take that off your head, you don't know who was wearing that.' Little did he know that I'd left it on the pump the previous night when walking a girl home; it had been getting in my way. I didn't tell Father this, but he took a dim view of me lifting the cap off the pump. If he had known the truth he may not have been any better pleased.

In any case, Banbridge Fair did the trick and it was the last time we had to take Old Brindle to market. The dealer from Portadown bought him. We did not get much money but we got a new home for him and we got the other cattle sold.

It wasn't until an old gentleman in Waco, Texas told me about the lead steers on the Chisholm Trail that I realised we had a valuable beast in Old Brindle. This old boy's grandfather rode on the Chisholm Trail, taking cattle to the rail heads and had a lead steer that led the droves through the rivers and creeks. When they got to the rail head they would turn the lead steer loose and it would go home again in time to bring the next drove. Very often it was home before the cowboys for they had a bit of socialising to do after they got to the rail-head and after the long drive. So Old Brindle was probably worth more for leading stock to market than he was to eat.

I probably showed the last Clydesdale horse at Banbridge Fair. After the Second World War, tractors were becoming more common and horses were being sold off in large numbers, many going for slaughter. I showed a three-year-old filly, Goldsprings Surprise, on the street in Banbridge in 1950. The only other horses on show that day were two ponies and a work horse. I sold the filly for £80 which was a good price for that time, about three times slaughter price. I was pleased she did not go to slaughter as she was a very nice filly having won first prize in her class at Newry Show. Her sire was Hill Statesman, a horse I had always admired and which belonged to a relation of mine, Robert Steele. The sire of Hill Statesman, Carries Air, had won the coveted Cawdor Cup at the Glasgow Stallion Show. So, good price or not, I was very relieved that our filly had found a new home.

I was probably one of the few young men at that time that mourned the passing of the horse as a way to farm. Most young ones of my age were keen on tractors and looking forward to the arrival of machinery. Although, like them, I eventually worked with tractors, it was just that, work. The day never went as quickly or enjoyably as it did when working with horses. And when you switched a tractor off it was dead. It was just a lump of steel. With horses it was different. As a boy going around and visiting friends and neighbours with my father and, when people came to visit us at Shanaghan, the ritual was that after tea or a meal, the men-folk would go out to inspect the horses. In the winter this meant going to the stables with the light from a tilly-lamp, but in the summer we would take a stroll across the fields to see the horses and maybe a young foal. Even if you had a £50,000 tractor sitting in the shed you would never think of taking your guests out to look it over. There was just something special about a horse. They were more or less part of the family on small farms at that time and great company. Much later when I was living in Scotland I bought myself a Clydesdale foal to enjoy that feeling one more time.

## Sarah & Keeper

I was having that Clydesdale foal shod one time in Scotland by a chap called Jacky Duffy that did all my shoeing when I lived over there, and happened to enquire if the Duffys had always been blacksmiths.

'No,' he said. 'Actually I served my time with an uncle. He was an Irishman being an uncle by marriage.'

'What part of Ireland did he come from?' I asked, mildly curious.

'A wee place in County Down called Katesbridge. His name was Bob Hillen,' he says as if it was a place too small for me to have heard of.

Now, I knew that family very well. Their blacksmith shop was at the end of Shanaghan Farm Lane. His sister Sarah ran a wee shop and a filling station there too and not being married lived in the same cottage as Bob was brought up in. The shop was a sort of meeting place for the village in the evening when the post office and only other shop in Katesbridge had closed. Sarah always kept her shop open until bedtime and a lot of folk, young and old, would congregate there for some conversation, especially in winter time around her wee, well stoked, log-burning stove. The older folk would play draughts or dominos, or take turns to scare the life out of us younger ones by telling us a lot of ghost stories. With Shanaghan Lane being a mile long and very, very dark if there was no moon to guide me, my imagination would see all sorts of things moving in the gloom on the long lonely walk home. Shivers would run up my spine if I heard any eerie sound – the worst of all being the unearthly call of a vixen.

Sarah had a mongrel dog called Keeper which was about the size of a border collie but with a curly coat. It was a dog that always impressed me and one of wisest I have ever seen. She could have sent it up to the cottage, about thirty yards from the shop, to fetch any number of things she would just ask for by name. I would often marvel at Keeper swivelling the long-handled broom to the vertical position to get it out the door and back down to the shop. If she sent him for the shovel he would have brought that instead. The fields surrounding the cottage were owned and farmed by the two Martin brothers, and they had a farm worker, Paddy Joe McArdle – actually the brother of Hugo McArdle the pig butcher who helped us in Shanaghan. If Paddy was out in the field, he could call Keeper and give him a few pence tucked up in a piece of paper. The dog knew to take this to Sarah and she knew to give Keeper a small packet of five Woodbine cigarettes to return to Paddy. Off Keeper would go with his package, tail in the air, back to the waiting Pat-Joe. Sarah just talked to Keeper like any other person and he seemed to know every word she said.

# The Good Life?

In Ireland back in the 'forties and 'fifties, we relied on the help of the local tradesmen as well as our neighbouring farmers, as there were always a few pork pigs to kill each week for the Monday market. We used two butchers, Hugh McGivern and Hugo McArdle. They usually worked together, but occasionally we would have got one of them, as they would work separately when busy. My father preferred to have Hugh McGivern as he used about half the amount of boiling water that the other butcher used to dress a pig.

Hugo, though, was quite a character. He told the story of a gentleman I knew well who had a squint in one eye and whom he had killed two pigs for. Knowing this man I could picture the scene. Anyway, while Hugo was killing the two pigs for him, the gentleman said to Hugo, 'Can I knock the second one down?' 'Certainly,' replies Hugo. So he snares the pig, brings it out and holds the rope for the man to hit the pig and stun it before it was bled. Not being so well acquainted with the man's squint, Hugo says, 'Hold on a minute. Are you for hitting where you're looking or looking where you're hitting for if you're hitting where you're looking I'm long enough here.'

During wartime a licence could be obtained from the government to kill a pig for your own family use. This was home-cured, put down in tea-chests and covered in salt. A little salt peter was used as well as far as I remember. After staying in the tea-chest for a few weeks it was taken out and hung on hooks from the kitchen ceiling. It was then ready to use during the winter and was really tasty bacon. In those days everyone was the farmer's friend. Even the local policemen beat a path to our door knowing they could always get a dozen eggs, a piece of home cured bacon, or a pound of butter.

A number of vacant houses were taken up by families evacuated to the country because of the bombing in Belfast.

Many only stayed for the duration of the war but others stayed on and settled in the country after the war was over. Some of these people would get themselves a goat and a few chickens. They were living the 'good life' and were quite self-sufficient.

Although these people were generally well liked and helped by the local community, there were a lot of tall stories told, poking fun at how little they knew about farming or animals. A story was told of a couple that bought a young sow thinking they could make a few pounds by selling young piglets and rear the odd one to kill for their own use. They enquired of the farmer how to get it to the boar to be mated. He told them that if they were to go out some morning and it appeared to be very tame, bring it up and mate it with his boar. One morning after this, it did indeed seem to be acting peculiar. When they put their hand on its back it stood still and tightened its ears. So they decided it was on heat and they would take it for mating.

This was more difficult to manage than they thought as the pig didn't want to come out of the paddock. After some thought

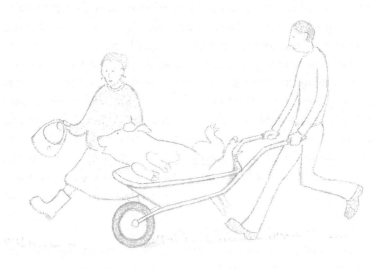

22

they decided to put it into the wheelbarrow and take it to the farm. So one held it in the barrow and the other wheeled. After a short distance it settled down quite well and when they got it to the farm they got it mated. The farmer said that if the sow was still in the same condition the next day to bring it back and he'd give it a second mating to make sure that there was a good litter, but as the next day was Sunday they'd have to be there before ten o'clock as he'd be going to church. In fact, they'd really need to be there by nine o'clock if possible.

The lady of the house was keen on the animals, and did the feeding. She looked out of the bedroom window the next morning to see how the sow was looking. Her husband says, 'I hope that old sow doesn't have to go to the farm today as I'm tired – we were late last night.' She says, 'Love, you're not going to believe this, but it's in the wheelbarrow.'

## Always There to Lend a Hand…

Although only a small place of a few hundred folk, Katesbridge could boast a tight-knit community. The blacksmith shop was a good meeting place. All the latest gossip could be heard there and you could easily get roped into helping out a neighbour if he had a job needing done.

There was a thriving linen industry in Ireland at that time and, as there was a lot of flax grown in that area, the flax mill in Katesbridge was a source of employment for many farm labourers during the winter months. Although flax was not grown at Shanaghan in my time, as a boy I would have been sent to help out our neighbours occasionally. At that time flax was pulled by hand, although in later years machines would do the job. After the flax was pulled it was put into bundles known as beats and tied with rush bands. I spent many days helping to make these rush bands before flax pulling started. Once pulled, it was then loaded on to the carts and drawn to flax dams full of water, which in some parts of the country were called Lint Holes. The flax was tramped down into the water in these Lint Holes and stones put on top to keep it weighed down for a few days until the outside coating was rotted. Once the flax was ready to come out of the water the stones were lifted off and the workers got in and began the heavy, dirty job of lifting each beat on to the bank. Farm carts were then loaded and the flax was drawn on to the fields, and once the bands were taken off each beat, the flax was spread thinly on the ground in rows. As there were no waterproofs, the workers would strip to the waist when working in the dam. With only a pair of boots and a pair of trousers, they'd be wet all day. When cleaning up in the evening after a day in the dam, the workmen would strip off in the byre or the stable and pour buckets of water over each other, then dry off and get into clean clothes ready for a night's entertainment.

Once the flax had dried out over the field, it was again tied into beats and built into stooks. There it would sit for some time before being drawn into the farm-steading and built in stacks to wait for the flax mill to take it in for 'scutching'. Everyone had to wait their turn as the mill was kept going all winter.

When the mill was ready, the flax was taken from the farm by horse and cart, each farmer sending some workers to help at the mill. There, the flax first went through the crimpers who used a roller to crack the outside of the flax and make it easier to remove the waste. From there it was passed to four workers we called 'streakers', although the real term is strickers. They twisted each bundle of flax over their arm and put it on a bench for the scutchers who beat it to soften the straw.

In Katesbridge Mill there were six scutchers all of whom were male, the strickers being women. The waste from the flax, known as 'shous', slang for shives, was wheeled to the fireman in the boiler house to feed the furnace and keep the mill's steam engine going. The flax fibre was tied into bundles by the scutchers and kept in the mill store to be collected for market in Banbridge where it was sold by the stone weight and priced according to quality.

Banbridge is a town built on the linen industry. At its peak it had five or six linen mills employing many people in the area, Irish linen being famous over the world. Ferguson's Mill in Banbridge is still operational and is the only place in the world that produces a special type of damask linen.

The environment in those old mills was very unhealthy with the workers toiling in the dust all day. It made me glad to be a farmer's boy working in the open air, whether that meant spreading manure by hand or not. Those days may be long gone, but you can still see a scutching mill in action at McConville's water-powered mill in Dromore, County Down, the last of its kind in Northern Ireland. Although practically all flax-making stopped in Ireland in the 1950s, Eugene McConville keeps his father's mill in full working order, raising his sluice gate to allow the waters of the River Lagan to turn the water wheel once more and keep an old craft alive.

## Neighbours, Characters and Nosey Parkers

On long summer evenings at that time folk gathered at crossroads and played quoits, using horseshoes from the blacksmith's shop to pitch over a peg maybe twenty yards away. A few nights later we'd meet up again to play marbles, throwing them until well after dark.

There was a telephone box at the cross-roads but not many of the older generation knew how to use the phone. No one had phones in the country then except for doctors, vets and ministers. When someone wanted to use the phone, usually only in an emergency, a lady, Hannah, who lived across the road from the phone box was always willing to give assistance. Apart from helping those unaccustomed to this new technology, she always liked to hear news from the country. There was not much that went on that she did not know about. In good weather she sat outside at the door knitting so as not to miss the opportunity of a chat with anyone who might be passing. At that time, and for a few years after the war, there were no road signs across the country so anyone not familiar with the area would have to ask directions. On one occasion while Hannah was sitting at her door, a car came screeching to a halt, a gentleman screwed down his window and yelled, 'Ma'am, where would that road to the left take me?'

'Sir, where would you be wanting to go?' she asks with a tilt of the head.

'Ah no place in particular,' he yells back, not wanting to give her too much information.

'Ah well,' she says getting on with her knitting, 'then any one of them will do you.'

In those days, if a girl had money or her father was wealthy she could get a husband without a problem, even if she wasn't too pretty. I was once told about a chap who had recently got married and who invited a friend to meet the new bride. He was no sooner introduced and drank his cup of tea than he was taken to see the new horse. This chap hadn't previously been in a position to keep a good horse and having now acquired one was very proud of it. When taking his friend into the stable to inspect and admire his new horse the new bride joined them. Not pleased that her new husband was more interested in showing off the horse than demonstrating affection for her, she says to his friend, 'If it had not been for my money that horse would not be here.'

'If it had not been for your money you wouldn't be here either,' he barked back, making her position crystal clear to all.

There were many characters like this in the country scratching out a meagre living. Others that spring to mind are a family not too far from Shanaghan that weren't too prosperous. There were two brothers and two sisters all living at home, all single and all trying to live off a small farm. With not too much money around, their farm-cart had long before worn out and for Saturday market days in Dromore they had made a habit of borrowing my grandfather's cart. If that cart was being used at harvest or any other busy time they would occasionally be able to borrow from some other neighbour. My uncle had reason to call on these people and when leaving, one of the sisters said, 'Show John the new cart in the shed.' When my uncle was admiring the new cart, the sister says with some satisfaction, 'We won't be needing your father's cart now, Johnnie.'

'And the Nelsons can go to Hell too,' shouts the other sister, which was perhaps a truer reflection of how they felt about their new–found independence.

## Local Worthies

When I was a young lad I knew an old guy called Wolf who travelled the countryside selling clothes. Guys like these were known as 'Packmen'. Wolf had a pony and trap which was further advanced than some others were. He called at a favourite meeting point, the Hawthorn Inn, frequently and sometimes had too much to drink. One Halloween night when he was in the pub, some boys at the crossroads decided to play a trick on him. They took the pony into the yard at the pub and put the shafts of the trap through the bars of the gate on the outside of the yard and yoked the pony on the inside. Wolf came out of the pub and looked at the pony and trap on each side of the gate. Says he, 'I've seen you in many a fix but how the heck you ever got yourself into that one beats me.'

The same old guy thought he would buy a cow so he rented a house and field not far from Banbridge. He decided to churn the milk and make butter so he got a lady to help. They both

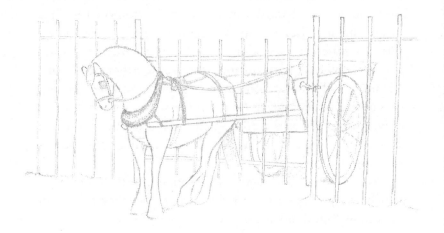

churned for hours but there was no sign of any butter. So he called in a farmer who was on his way home from market to see what the problem could be. The farmer looked at him and said, 'Mr Wolf, she maybe isn't a butter cow, maybe she's a cheese cow.' We roared with laughter at that story then but recently I was reading in the *Scottish Farmer* that scientists in America have genetically modified a cow to be more suitable for producing cheese than butter. Little did the farmer realise that there just might be a cheese cow one day.

Another story is told of a local worthy who was taken into hospital in Banbridge. He had never been far travelled before and he had certainly never been in hospital. He was suffering a lot of pain and the doctor asked him had he urinated recently. Old Robert looked a bit quizzically at the doctor and says, 'What would you be meaning now, Doctor?' So the doctor tries again and asked if he had passed any water recently. 'Ah I see, well now,' says Robert. 'I did to be sure. I passed the Corbett Lough coming in,' which is a lough between Katesbridge and Banbridge hospital.

With money quite tight, farmers were very, very superstitious and any bad luck with stock would be put down to someone putting a curse on them or bewitching them. Stories were often told about the antics of some of these superstitious old men, especially an old guy and neighbouring farmer who my grandfather took me to see when I was a boy of three or four. This old boy, Alec was his name, was so superstitious that he would not trim back any of the hawthorn bushes growing wild in the middle of his fields as these were 'fairy thorns' and to cut them at all would be very bad luck.

One time one of his horses dropped dead unexpectedly and he was told that the horse must have been bewitched. Someone advised him to burn the dead horse and he would probably get the witch too. When the horse was burning some smart guy came with the skeleton of a cat and placed it carefully between the remains of the horse's front legs.

Next day when Alec was in the village he was telling all he met that he had got the witch and that his luck would be turning. When folk asked him what the witch was like he told them in hushed tones and in all seriousness that it was 'cat-like'. That story was told for a long time across the country at the expense of old Alec, but the superstitions raged on.

## Where There's a Will...

My grandfather was Executor for many of the local farmers' wills which the local clergyman would have written, so we always had a lot of copies of wills in the house, some of which made interesting reading. The amount on one receipt for a wake and a funeral was £4.2s.6d. with a discount of 2s. 6d., which seemed generous. The writing was perfect copybook and signed over a halfpenny stamp. That account included an oak coffin with brass mountings, a shroud, a hearse and two horses (apparently a one-horse hearse was cheaper), seven pounds of cheese, two kegs of wine, and one and half gallons of whiskey – the whiskey cost twenty-seven shillings which works out at eighteen shillings a gallon or ninety pence in today's currency.

The arrangements made in these wills for those left behind were fairly Spartan. Many of the farmers' wills had a provision that, when they died, their widow would be left a room in the house and an allocation of oatmeal, potatoes, milk and butter. If she remarried, she could get £5 and had to leave the premises. I somehow don't think this arrangement would work today. Not many would settle for £5, which in the late 1880s was the price of a cow. A cow today of that standard would be around £800 to £1000, non-pedigree.

It wasn't just the wills that seem a bit far fetched, there were also the characters who seemed to make a profession out of attending the wakes – a social gathering and payment of respects which would last from the death to the burial. No one seemed to go to bed. There would be plenty of food and drink and pipes and tobacco for the smokers.

My father told about an old man called Jack White who would visit all the wakes in the country, making a living out of helping out on the farms, feeding cattle, or whatever was needed during the days of the wake. After coming home from having travelled a fairly long distance on one occasion, he found out that his next door neighbour had died and was already buried. 'He was an awkward bugger all his life and he died awkward,' was all Jack had to say about it.

## Cycling through County Down

Most of my young days were spent around the market town of Banbridge in County Down. Banbridge can also boast a few famous ancestors. That includes the Bronte sisters, whose father Patrick was a pastor and schoolteacher in Drumballyroney Church, not far away. And then there's Captain Crozier who was lost in an expedition to the North West Passage and who is commemorated by a large monument in Church Square. Yet another is Joseph Scriven who wrote the hymn 'What a friend we have in Jesus', the words of which are inscribed on his memorial in the town.

There's also a famous song about Banbridge town in the County Down which I was once surprised to hear being sung round a fire in the United States of America. So for a modest town, it's one that has made its presence felt.

### The Star of the County Down

Near Banbridge Town,
In the County Down
One morning last July,
Down a *búithrin* green
Came a sweet colleen,
And she smiled as she passed me by.
She looked so neat
From her bare brown feet
To the sheen of her nut-brown hair,
Such a coaxing elf,
Sure, I shook myself
To make sure I was standing there

*Chorus*

*From Bantry Bay*
*Up to Derry Quay*
*And from Galway to Dublin Town*
*No maid I've seen*
*Like the brown colleen*
*That I met in the County Down*

As she onward sped,
Sure I turned my head
And I gazed with a feeling rare.
And I says, says I, to a passer by:
'Who's the maid with the nut-brown hair?'
He smiled at me
And he says, says he,
'That's the gem of old Ireland's crown.
Sweet Rosey McCann
From the banks of the Bann,
She's the Star of the County Down.'

*Chorus*

She'd a soft brown eye
And a look so sly
And a smile like the rose in June
And you hung on each note
From her lily-white throat
As she lilted an Irish tune.
At the pattern dance
You were held in a trance
As she tripped through a reel or a jig;
And when her eyes she'd roll,
She'd coax, on my soul,
A spud from a hungry pig.

*Chorus*

I've travelled a bit
But I never was hit
Since my roving career began;
But fair and square
I surrendered there
To the charms of sweet Rose McCann.

I'd a heart to let
And no tenant yet
Though I'd searched countryside and town;
But in she went,
And I asked no rent
From the Star of the County Down.

*Chorus*

At the harvest fair
She'll be surely there
So I'll dress in my Sunday clothes.
With my shoes shone bright
And my hat cocked right
For a smile from my nut-brown Rose.
No horse I'll yoke,
No pipe I'll smoke
Though my plough with the rust turn brown,
Till a smiling bride
By my own fire side
Sits the Star of the County Down.

*Chorus*

During my teenage and early years there was a lot of
night life in Banbridge with four dance halls where good
live music was always played. There was also a cinema where
two shows were held each night, first and second house, and
three different films shown during the week. With this level
of entertainment Banbridge was a popular place with the
younger generation and on Saturday night, late trains would
run to cater for the dancers and cinema-goers. When coming
home late at night I would hear people whistling the latest
tunes. I don't hear whistling nowadays. In my day when a car
went by going 'bump, bump, bump' it had a flat wheel. Today

it's the music that goes 'bump, bump, bump'. It doesn't really sound like music to whistle to.

When I was around sixteen years old I joined Banbridge Cycle Club, following some of my friends who'd joined earlier and went on to cycle with the club and race for about five years. I really enjoyed the training which involved riding through the Mourne Mountains, the most picturesque mountain district in Ireland – to this day over eighty square miles of unspoilt mountain and moorland. There are twelve peaks, ten of which are over two thousand feet high, Slieve Donard being the tallest. It is an area close to the heart of all Irish people and has been immortalised in the words of Percy French's song '...where the Mountains o' Mourne sweep down to the sea'.

### The Mountains of Mourne

Oh Mary this London's a wonderful sight
With people here workin' by day and by night
They don't sow potatoes, nor barley, nor wheat
But there's gangs of them diggin' for gold in the street
At least when I asked them that's what I was told
So I just took a hand for this diggin' for gold
But for all that I found there I might as well be
Where the Mountains of Mourne sweep down to
    the sea.

I believe that when writin' a wish you expressed
As to how the fine ladies in London were dressed
Well if you'll believe me, when asked to a ball
They don't wear no top to their dresses at all
Oh I've seen meself and you could not in truth
Say if they were bound for a ball or a bath
Don't be startin' them fashions, now Mary McCree
Where the Mountains of Mourne sweep down to
    the sea.

There's beautiful girls here, oh never you mind
With beautiful shapes nature never designed
And lovely complexions all roses and cream
But let me remark with regard to the same
That if that those roses you venture to sip
The colours might all come away on your lip
So I'll wait for the wild rose that's waitin' for me
In the place where the dark Mournes sweep down
    to the sea.

I would cycle around sixty miles, training three or four times each week, making sure I took in as much of the Mournes as I could. It was particularly good in the springtime when the lambs were playing through the fields and mountains. When you cycle through the countryside you hear the birds singing and smell the hedges and flowers, whereas when driving a car you have the picture but no sound or smell. I used to hear larks singing in the evening when I was cycling – a sound not to be heard anywhere around here now. There were also corncrakes in almost every hay field. I haven't heard a corncrake for many years – maybe down to modern farming, an over population of foxes, or both.

I enjoyed racing and on one occasion my uncle took me and my friend, Stanley Thompson, to a race in Dublin where there was an entry of about one hundred. The race was from Phoenix Park to Cavan Town and back, a distance of 140 miles which we completed in six hours. About ten miles after the start I got a puncture and had to wait for my uncle coming behind in the car to get the wheel changed. I had to ride ten miles to catch up with the race and then felt the need to rest up with the bunch for a time.

My friend Stanley got stomach cramp on the way back from Cavan Town and called on my uncle for something to help. My uncle and another friend from the cycle club were following in a car, and had been given responsibility for our food and drinks. In a bit of a fuss they managed to give Stanley my drink of Lucozade and me Stanley's cramp mixture. That turned out to be brandy. It could just as well have been rocket fuel for it propelled me to the front of the bunch for most of the way back. Any attempts by the others to break away found me with them. It's a great pity I wasn't administered a second dose of this mixture about five miles from the finish. I was in the front row of the bunch coming into Phoenix Park but I finished three seconds behind the winner to be in twelfth place, the winner being the English Champion named Tiny Thomas. He went on a short time afterwards to win second in the World Championship.

A later race that comes to mind which didn't have a happy ending was the Festival of Britain Race in Lurgan, a race of about one hundred competitors. After getting my bike passed by the scrutiniser, my back brake cable snapped leaving me with only a front brake. I should not have started the race but being young and foolish I decided to go ahead. It was a damp and drizzly day which makes racing more dangerous.

On the first lap of the hundred kilometre race (around sixty two miles) and while coming down a steep hill, I heard a racket up front which I knew was a pile-up. As this was a narrow road there was no way of avoiding the crash and, as I had only one brake, I hit the pile much faster than the others, flying right over the pile and landing on a grass verge. I picked myself up, amazingly without injury. My bike though was a complete write- off, the front wheel was nearly touching the back one.

As we were around two miles from town I put the bike over my shoulder and walked back to the dressing rooms. There was a St John's Ambulance following the race but it was full to the rafters with injured riders, sixteen or seventeen needing hospital treatment. As I carried the bent-up bike past the spectators they were looking at me, nodding over and laughing. I supposed it was because of the state of the bicycle so I just laughed back. It was only when I got to the dressing room that I twigged that their amusement was more to do with the state of my shorts. My bare backside had been hanging out the whole walk back having been torn asunder in the crash. In the excitement I mustn't have felt the cold.

My racing career came to an end at the age of twenty-one as a result of an injured ankle – or maybe it was as much to do with meeting a redhead, Wilma, who distracted me from my training nights. Wilma later became my wife and mother to my four children, our eldest son Alan, the twins Jeff and Jennifer and our youngest, Joanne. They were a fairly ragamuffin bunch up there on Shanaghan Farm in those early days and, being a mile up a lane from Katesbridge, their playmates were most usually, like mine when I was their age, the working or retired border collies around the yard.

I still look back on my cycling years as some of my most enjoyable. It certainly kept my weight down, I was around nine to ten stone at that time which quickly rose to fifteen stone when I stopped – the weight I've remained ever since. To this day I'm in contact with the friends I made in those few years of cycling. And of course, as in the words of the song, I've had my very own Star of the County Down by my fireside.

# The Border Collie

As you've probably gathered by now, I have a special respect for the working sheepdog or Border Collie which is pretty much the unsung hero of any livestock farm. A good dog literally does the work of ten men – and in much better humour. While some lowland farmers have more recently resorted to quad bikes, at great expense, to help manage their stock, they more often than not have a sheepdog riding on it with them – the dog being there for the difficult tasks. And of course, a quad bike is useless on a hill farm. There the border collie just can't be replaced. It's hard to describe the pleasure of working with a dog that is listening and responding to whistle commands at distances of more than half a mile away on a windswept hill. In fact, it's worth considering for a minute that without the border collie, huge tracts of rough, mountainous terrain across the world could not be farmed and would be left unproductive.

So where did this breed come from? It was back in the 1900s when the name 'Border Collie' was first used in the border country of England and Scotland to define a type of working dog that was being bred for their intelligence and instinct in managing stock, not for their appearance. For that reason they tend to vary quite a bit in physical appearance – but a good handler knows the qualities he or she is looking for.

Being an only son on a mainly arable and stock farm I found time to develop my own very straightforward way of communicating with the dogs my father kept. My first dog, Cap, like most border collies, was very keen to please. We built up a great friendship before I began to teach him a few commands to help me at work. When he understood what I was trying to say and he knew I was pleased, he would jump up to let me know he was glad to have been of help and had enjoyed himself. We had achieved something together. That was the fun. And that has been the basis of everything I have done with working sheepdogs ever since. Working with them in partnership.

What had begun as a game between Cap and me soon became my lifelong passion, biasing me towards sheep farming and inevitably, sheepdog trials. My close relationship with my dogs as a handler and the relatively simple approach I have taken to training and building a language of commands, all stem from the ease of that early friendship with Cap.

Although Cap was a great and memorable dog, my first registered puppy was Fly which I bought from my neighbour Jimmy Crothers and brought home in the saddle bag of my bike.

Jimmy was not only a sheepdog man, he was also a very good horseman and a leading point to point jockey. He's still a keen horseman to this day and has been a close friend all my life. Fly shared the same father as Cap, but unlike Cap's mother who was just a farm dog, Jimmy had Fly's mother, 'Maid' registered. I now had my first bone fide sheepdog to try to train in earnest. I didn't realise that my journey home on the racing bike was the start of a whole new way of life.

## My First Sheepdog Trial

As my cycling came to an end, I began to have my first success at sheepdog trials. I had grown up with border collies and saw how much my father depended on them to work the farm. I had a very close relationship with Cap, and went on from there to train my first real working dog, Dick. Shanaghan was more than a sheep farm but I found myself spending more and more time with the dogs.

In 1952, at the age of twenty-two, I took the plunge and entered Dick in my first sheepdog trial, held at a horse fair in Banbridge. This was a fairly high-profile trial classed as an Open Trial, which is one where the contestants compete for points towards entry into the annual National Championship organised each year by the International Sheepdog Society. I thought I might at the very least pick up a few tips from the recognised experts of the day. My dog handling technique was very much home-made; a way of communicating which I'd worked out between me and my few dogs.

Dick won the Novice Class that day (that is against dogs which have not yet won a prize in an Open Trial) and was third in the Open Trial itself. I wasn't surprised Dick could run that well, I just hadn't had the chance to compare how we worked against other dogs and handlers before. The talk at the edge of the course was that it was beginner's luck but a promising start nonetheless. I thought no more about it until a few days later when I had a visit from A P Wilson of Rich Hill, one of the top trial men in Ireland at that time. We struck a bargain and he went away a happy man having bought Dick for fifty pounds – ten times a man's weekly wage at that time and the talk of the country for a long time afterwards. That was me hooked and sheepdog handling and trials have been central to everything I've done ever since.

*Early trophies on display for a local journalist on the lawn at Shanaghan*

# WINNING WAYS

## A Special Dog, Nell

My first really good sheepdog trial win came at Ardee in 1956 with a dog called Nell. I had bought Nell as a puppy of eight weeks old, paying eight pounds for her and her carriage from Auchterarder in Perthshire to Katesbridge station. She was the daughter of a famous Scottish dog, David Murray's Vic.

Of all the dogs I have trained and run, Nell remains a great favourite of mine. When she was only about eleven months old, Sammy Holmes and I decided we would go to Slieve Donard one Boxing Day to gather up some sheep and give the dogs a bit of a run. Slieve Donard is the highest peak in the Mournes at 2,700 feet high.

It was Nell's first time being on the mountain and it was blowing a gale. Towards the evening there were sheep quite high out on the face of the mountain and by then we were down in the bottom of the glen. Says Sammy, 'There's a good run for the young bitch.' So I put her up the mountain but some of the sheep must have been grazing on the other side and when the few sheep on our side saw the dog coming they disappeared over the ridge. With the gale Nell could not hear me calling her to come back, so she went over the ridge after the sheep and out of sight. We called and called but she never came back and by now it was getting very dark. So Sammy says, 'You head up towards the tower at the top of the ridge one way and I'll head up the other way and we'll see if we can spot her. We wouldn't want to leave her out all night.'

It was a long, slow climb to the tower and when we both arrived it was six o'clock and pitch dark. Neither of us had found her despite whistling all the way up. So with a heavy heart I headed off back down into the glen with Sammy, following the glen river down to the forest and then working our way slowly through the forest in the dark to the forestry road. When we got to the Land Rover, Nell was sitting in the back waiting for us to return. I remember Sammy saying to me then, 'You've got something special there, look after her.' And sure enough she had a very bright future.

When she was only about a year old I took her to compete at Hyde Park in London at the Daily Express Trials. These were held on Whit weekend with a trial on the Saturday and another on Monday. In this particular year the dogs were kennelled in the Barracks of the Royal Horseguards in Knightsbridge. There was a row of twenty or thirty horse boxes or stables down both

sides of a long yard and Nell was kennelled in the very last horse box on the left where she slept for two nights. It was two years before she was back again to Hyde Park for this Daily Express Trial. As soon as we arrived at the gate of the yard, I slipped the lead off her and, without hesitation, she went galloping off to the bottom left hand box and jumped in over the door. She had no sooner jumped in than she had to jump out again, for there was a horse in that box that year.

Her first really big chance to shine was at a trial in Ardee in County Louth sponsored by the Irish Tourist Board. There was always a high entry for that trial and so when I had tried to enter the competition the year before in 1955, I received a letter back from the secretary to say that, as there were a large number of competitors coming from England, Scotland and Wales, they were only taking entries from 'established Irish handlers'. They told me to try again in 1956 which I did. This time I got a reply to say that owing to the large entry they weren't sure whether there would be enough time to let me run, but to come anyway and if I didn't get a run they would refund my entry fee.

When we arrived at the trial apparently there had been a very good run put up by a famous English handler. At that time we were judged out of fifty points and as the English handler had managed to keep a total of forty-eight points, there wasn't much room for me to improve on his run. Despite the warning that I might not be able to run I had taken two dogs with me, Nell and Susie. In my entry I had explained that if there was only time for me to run one dog I would run Nell, but if there was time for two I would run Susie first. As it turned out they let me go ahead with the two dogs.

So Susie took to the field, ran well and came away with forty seven points, putting her in second place. A reporter came up to me when I had finished to see if I had been trialling long, asked about my dogs and how I thought I would do with Nell. 'Well Nell always beats Susie,' I replied straight away, maybe a wee bit peeved for not being allowed to enter the year before and being young and a bit cocky.

It wasn't long before I had the chance to test those words. I walked out with Nell and we completed the run well. To my mind, I had bettered the run I'd had with Susie. All around the field the competitors and spectators were interested and waiting to see how I would fare with the judges. When my score was put up it was forty-nine and a half.

For that win I was presented with a trophy to keep by the Tourist Board and twenty pounds, which in 1956 was two weeks' wages or the price of a decent dog.

It was two years later, in 1958 that I won my first National title in Bangor, County Down with Nell and in 1963, Nell, together with another dog I had called Pete, won the Irish Brace Championship. Before 1961 Irish Nationals were organised by the Northern Ireland Sheepdog Association. In 1961, when the organisation was taken over by the International Sheepdog Society, they allowed only three dogs with the highest points to go forward to the International Championships. By 1965 we had an all-Ireland National including handlers from Eire and the Isle of Man and were making a much bigger impression.

That dog Nell and I had been together since she was a pup of only eight weeks old and she went on to win trials all her life, winning her last at eleven years old.

## Sport or Trial?

The stories I tell write about sheepdogs and trials, and any tips I give along the way, all stem from the need I had, in common with most shepherds, for a dog I could communicate and work with easily on the farm – a dog I could trust to use its own intelligence. Anyone who owns a dog, sheepdog or not, wants a relatively simple way to train it and

I think there's a fair amount to be learnt from the training of the border collie for working and trial conditions.

Border collies are bred to be working dogs and need careful training to bring out their natural talent so that they can be relied upon in real working situations. Those who train dogs for a working life on the farm are always keen to test the skill of their dogs against others and learn from other handlers. The Sheepdog Trial grew out of this need.

Sheepdog trial courses were mainly set out by renowned handlers such as the late Sandy Millar, J M Wilson, William Wallace and the Telford brothers of the North of England. These men did a very good job. The courses they designed have stood the test of time and are universal in sheepdog trials the world over.

The basic trial run involves a set of sheep (usually five) being released to stand at a Post at the top of the course, three or four hundred yards from the handler and dog. The handler sends the dog away from his side to pick up or 'Lift' the sheep and the action the dog takes in sweeping around, ideally unseen, to arrive just behind them is referred to as the 'Outrun'.

If the Lift is a good one the sheep will start to move gently off the Post in a straight line down the course towards the handler, going through a set of gates on the way. This is the Fetch. Once close to the handler, the task is to complete what is called the 'Drive' – a sort of an inverted triangular shape, each side being around 150 yards long and requiring the dog to manoeuvre the sheep in as straight a line as possible through two sets of gates on the way – more or less on each of the upper corners of the triangle. Now is the time for the Pen – the most often photographed part of the trial, where the dog is required to coax the sheep into a small fenced-in enclosure. The party trick of one very famous dog, Willie Dunn's Roy, at this point was to close the gate of the pen with his two front paws, but no more points are awarded for this sort of showmanship. Finally, once released from their Pen, the sheep are brought to a marked out circle, the Shedding Ring, about forty feet in diameter, where the dog is given a command to 'Shed' or separate some of the sheep from the others. Usually two of the five sheep sport coloured ribbons and the dog may be asked to separate or Shed just one of these sheep – often referred to as the Single Shed. A standard scoring system has been established by the International Sheepdog Society allocating marks to each of these sections of the course. Points can be lost for mistakes made around the course, at the discretion of the judge. The highest score wins.

Although the course is more or less the same, each trial still manages to be different with various types of ground and sheep. Some courses are on open hill ground and some are in fenced enclosures. Some sheep are light, easy to move, and some are heavy, or stubborn. All trials share, or should share, the original purpose as established by the International Sheepdog Society back in 1906 – to test and improve the skills of the handler and working dog in the management of their stock.

As sheepdog trialling is now a worldwide sport with a high percentage of handlers enjoying it purely for fun, it is more and more important that competitors come to a trial for the right reasons. That is, understanding that it is a test of their practical skills as a handler and of their dog's ability to control sheep in a simulation of a working environment. If it is approached just as a competition, or worse, as some form of dog obedience test, then I see a real danger for the future integrity of sheepdog trials and for the quality of the dogs being bred.

More and more judges at sheepdog trials also fall into what could be called the 'hobbyist' category, interested and enthusiastic about trials as a form of sport but perhaps not having a deeper practical base to inform their decisions. The danger for these judges is that they can be inclined to judge trials without sufficient reference to the severity of a fault in a working situation and so are in danger of focusing too heavily on technical misdemeanours, penalising and rewarding the wrong dogs and so jeopardising the trial's relevance and fairness.

Without continued focus from judges on the practical merits and faults of a trial run, there is likely to be more and more demand for dogs bred especially for their obedience, but not necessarily their intelligence or control of the sheep. The danger of this trend could be that we lose the type of dog that has natural working ability and so have fewer and fewer useful dogs for the reality of hill and farm work. As an example, many of the top modern handlers prefer dogs that are very highly trained, that do just as they are told and are not able to run out to the sheep in a smooth wide curve without the sheep seeing it, sweeping round to be just behind them in a way that is both natural and effective in getting the sheep to move towards the handler. In sheepdog trial circles we call a dog that can do this a 'natural Outrunner'. Yet, rather than rely on the talent of the dog in Outrunning, some handlers train the Outruns onto them, steering them with whistles all the way. I can understand this because a dog that you train to run out to the sheep according to a very tight set of commands in a trial environment can be controlled in his lines to the sheep – and, as it currently stands, may win the trial as a result. But the weakness in this practice is that, because they win trials, they are being used as stud dogs to the extent that we are breeding obedient dogs, not necessarily those with natural ability and intellect.

This has made me think that it might be time to look again at the sheepdog trial format and rules of judging. I think we need to redress the balance and find a way to reward and so increase the appreciation of dogs demonstrating the ability and skill to think and act for themselves to the benefit of the handler:dog partnership. There are areas which in my view could be revised to really test the dog and handler in their ability to work together as a team in managing the sheep. I like the idea of the 'Silent Gather', where the dog is tested in its ability to bring the sheep to you with no commands. And I'm really not sure we need to put so much emphasis these days on the action that takes place in the Shedding Ring. I pick up on these suggestions later when I explain how I went about training one of my best dogs, Dick. I'm not suggesting that these are the right or only options, just a bit of starter for the kind of debate that I think is needed at this stage in the development of the sport – and before the pressures of competition overtake the underlying principles of trialling.

## The Sheepdog Trial Hierarchy

Open Trials are run locally to allow handlers to gain points towards entry to the National trial – limited in each of the Irish, Scottish, Welsh and English Nationals to the 150 handlers and their dogs with the highest points. To my mind, however, this system of points creates a problem in that it favours those handlers who are able to compete in a high quantity of Open trials each season. Handlers who have farming commitments and so do not have the time to travel to and compete in such a high number of trials are therefore at an obvious disadvantage. I would prefer a system in which handlers nominate ten trials to compete in at the beginning

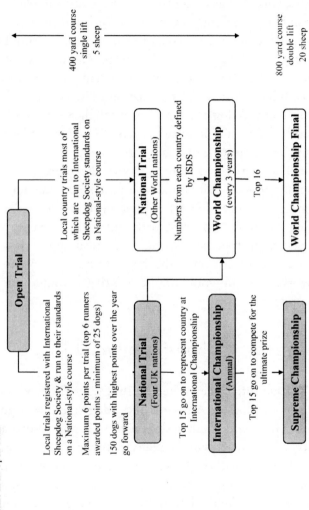

**Nursery Trials**

Dogs under 3 years old which have not won a prize in an Open Trial

**Open Trial**

Local trials registered with International Sheepdog Society & run to their standards on a National-style course

Maximum 6 points per trial (top 6 runners awarded points - minimum of 25 dogs)

150 dogs with highest points over the year go forward

Local country trials most of which are run to International Sheepdog Society standards on a National-style course

**National Trial** (Other World nations)

Numbers from each country defined by ISDS

**National Trial** (Four UK nations)

Top 15 go on to represent country at International Championship

**International Championship** (Annual)

Top 15 go on to compete for the ultimate prize

**Supreme Championship**

**World Championship** (every 3 years)

Top 16 →

**World Championship Final**

400 yard course
single lift
5 sheep

800 yard course
double lift
20 sheep

of the season, with their top three scores counting towards qualification for the National.

These Open trials are run according to the International Sheepdog Society standard for the National Trial itself, with handlers competing over a 400-yard course with five sheep and containing the standard elements of Outrun, Lift, Fetch, Drive, Shed, Pen and Single Sheep. The ultimate stage of the International trial is the Supreme Championship, involving the last fifteen dogs in the four nations. The course and so test on the handler/dog team becomes tougher, stretching over 800 yards and including what's called a "Double Lift" – picking up and working with two sets of ten sheep.

There are some calls to reduce the number of sheep, but in my opinion that would be a mistake. To adjudge a supreme champion sheepdog, I think we need to see evidence of the dog being able to work with and control twenty sheep and keep them together. Taking a practical approach, a dog that cannot control twenty sheep would be of no use in everyday working – and would not be one that I would want to have a puppy from.

## Choosing a Good Dog

I have often been asked to find dogs for folk and to send good dogs to America. Sheepdog trials are a good shop-window for finding dogs with style and natural ability and to make contact with handlers that will have puppies available.

Every year though, we seem to have more dog dealers for purely trial dogs, with the result that less responsible trainers are mass producing half-trained sheepdogs over a short period of time to sell to these dealers and at dog auctions. This is really only a money-making practice. Sheepdogs cannot be mass-produced. They need time to develop. They are individuals and should be treated accordingly to bring out their natural ability.

So how do you find a good dog?

Not all border collies, no matter how they're bred, are good trial or working dogs, although often 'dud' dogs from good parents go on to breed some top class dogs.

It takes about two and half years to train a dog and around three hundred hours of instruction, which can add up to a fairly big expense. So before investing time and money on training a dog, you need to try to make sure you pick one showing glimmers of its natural ability. As they say, 'You can't make a gem out of a lump of glass,' so it pays to know what to look for in a puppy before you start.

As far as family history or breeding goes, to many people, a top class sheepdog is one that has a lot of international champions in its pedigree. I prefer to know that there are a number of dogs in its ancestry that are of the type and have the working qualities I like – natural balance and intelligence when working with sheep. Each handler has their own view of what are good working qualities, but I like a dog that can get in behind the sheep, take control, and drive them where he wants them to go. Too many dogs simply walk behind the sheep if they are going in the right direction, but they can't make things happen; they don't have the right authority over their sheep.

At the World Trials in Tullamore, County Offaly in Ireland in 2005, I was very impressed with a dog called Fleet which a Swedish handler had trained. Fleet's method of working sheep was very self-assured. I watched him in the qualifying rounds when he had to work five sheep and I said to myself, 'If that dog can work with twenty sheep the way he can with these five, it's one of the best dogs I've ever seen.' That dog made it to the final and finished up sixth in the world. He was working twenty Suffolk sheep which most of the dogs in the Final were struggling to push round the course in the heat, but he was able to push them round just the same as he had been able to push the five sheep round. When I checked the programme and looked at his breeding, he was by Johnny Wilson's Rob, a dog with a very good reputation but one I had never actually seen work myself. I then noticed, however, his mother was Gail, a bitch of Donald MacDonald's and a daughter of one of my best dogs, Dick. So this dog I'd been attracted to was actually a grandson of Dick. His value was clear to me, not from his pedigree, which I didn't know until I began to make enquiries, but by his manner of working. To me he was the dog of the trial and when I found out more about him, he was actually the European Champion. To my mind this is the sort of dog that should be made a lot of use of as a stud dog and which would produce a good blood line.

When looking at the appearance of the puppy and its parents, bear in mind that working border collies come in different sizes and with different coats. Some have what we call bear-skin short coats and some are long haired, with rough or medium coats. There is no fixed colour. Some are black and white, some are black, white and tan, some have blue-mottle on their legs, some have quite a bit of white and some have almost no white. Sometimes we get brown dogs which can be quite good working dogs but it is not a wanted colour. Brown dogs seem to attract sheep and find them harder to move. The same goes for a pure white dog. No one wants a pure white dog. While he may have the working qualities, the sheep don't seem to move off a white dog so well and at lambing time the lambs will follow a white dog rather than their mothers.

Two very important characteristics of a working border collie are their head carriage and tail carriage. You can tell more about the temperament of a border collie by his tail than any other part of his body. When he is working, a border collie's tail should be carried, without movement, quite close to his hind legs. When you see a dog flicking his tail about when working, or raising his tail up high, this is mostly a sign of weakness. So handlers put a lot of importance on tail carriage especially.

Head carriage should be low to the ground, like a lion stalking his prey. Sheep seem to be better at moving off a dog which has low head carriage. If a dog's head carriage is a bit high, it might not affect the working ability so much but the dog will be classed as a 'plain dog'. A stylish dog keeps his head low to the ground and his tail tucked down while he is working.

In terms of physique, the type of dog I like to own is one with a good broad skull and a high brow – plenty of room for brains. I do not like a dog with a long narrow head, a long back or an overly long tail. Often a dog with a very long tail has got a bend to one side at the end of its tail. It may seem like a strange observation but over the years I have noticed that long-backed and long-tailed dogs do not stand as much work in warm weather.

For me, what it all boils down to is that a good dog is one that can cope well in an everyday working environment. I would not breed off, or buy a puppy from, a dog that could not handle twenty sheep as eventually you would create a strain of dog that would be too light and would be of no use for everyday working.

Different people have different ideas about what 'power' is in a dog. To me, a powerful dog is one that can walk steadily up to the head of the sheep, the leader of the flock, and if the lead sheep is aggressive and 'goes for him', the dog stands steady rather than give ground or run back. Many folk seem to be of the opinion that a dog that rushes on and continues to push the sheep has too much power for trialling. I have found over the years that many of these dogs that rush on are actually weak dogs which are afraid of the sheep stopping and cannot stand steady when the sheep are facing up to them.

To me the proper working or trial dog is a dog with lots of power which he hides from the sheep until it's needed.

Despite the variations in trial conditions, good dogs can size up the different situations they face. In my experience, good dogs usually get good sheep. I hear some folk say, 'My dog is very unlucky, I'm sure to get bad sheep.' But I have noticed over the years that the sheep could be terrible, with everyone complaining but when a good dog goes out (one that comes to mind is Bobby Dalziel's Joe), the sheep are just fine. A good dog senses his sheep and is able to give the sheep confidence. He takes good care and, as they say, 'Good care always eats the heels of bad luck.'

So if you summarise all this for what to look for in a puppy, I would say – look at the working qualities of the parents or grandparents. Do they demand the respect of the sheep they are working? Can they work more than twenty sheep calmly and with relative ease? Are they stylish dogs, with low tail and head carriage? I would try to buy from a mating of two such

dogs, ideally if I had already seen that they can produce good pups. Otherwise I would look for a bitch from a good bloodline which had consistently produced good pups, whether or not she was a good trial dog herself.

If you find what you believe should be a good litter, don't rush into a choice. When choosing your puppy, usually best from the age of ten weeks' old, look for glimmerings of those characteristics that make a good dog as well as for one that has a pleasant, sociable nature. By that I mean one that is not too nervous, but which is curious enough to come up to say hello, and while confident in playing with its brothers and sisters, is maybe a bit more interested in the outside world than the rest of them. One of my very best dogs, Dick was always wandering away from the litter when he was a pup and his son Cap was even worse. I had a dreadful time trying to keep Cap together with his mother and the rest of the litter at night. No matter how securely I thought I had the kennels closed, Cap would always have found a way to wriggle out into the yard. Not being so adept at getting back into the warmth of the kennel, I'd more often than not find him sitting at the door like a wee drowned rat in the morning. That dog became one of my best trial dogs.

Then again, there may be one that sits back and sort of sizes up the situation. I always had a bit of a liking for that type of puppy, as long as it didn't run away when it saw a stranger. I thought it was using its brain a wee bit.

Once you have made your choice from the litter, take time to get to know the dog before launching into training. Look for the dog's strengths and weaknesses and take time to think about how you will need to work with that dog to help it understand what you want it to do – only then will your commands make any sense. Dogs do not think like humans do, and every dog thinks differently, so it is important to have patience in finding the best way to explain to the dog what you want him to do, rather than imposing your will as his "master". Having found a good dog, it's a dreadful waste to rely solely on your own ability. No matter who you are, often the dog's a lot smarter when it comes to working sheep.

## Who's in Charge?

A sheepdog is part of a team and good as he may be, he also relies on the skills and temperament of his handler. Not all International Sheepdog Championships have been won by outstanding dogs, but what they all have in common is a top class handler who knows how to work together with the dog to best effect.

It is always good to see a dog worked quietly, the handler keeping calm and not getting flustered when situations go wrong. A good handler never corrects a dog for doing wrong until he is quite certain the dog knows how to carry out the task properly. A good handler can also tell the difference between hard nature and soft nature dogs and be able to work with either type – if he can manage this he will never be without a dog. A hard nature dog needs to be handled firmly but quietly. With a soft nature dog, you need to give him the impression that he is beating you – and then he will give you of his best – horse jockeys will understand this.

There has been a lot written about how a sheepdog handler can gain the respect of his dogs. Many liken the handler to the 'pack leader'. Some say dogs are descended from the wolf and in the wild their instinct is to obey the pack leader. But I think the handler-sheepdog relationship is more complicated than that. Wolves hunt in packs, a sheepdog works one to one with the handler. The pack leader instils authority by force, the rest of the pack obey him and are rewarded by feeding all down the line, the most timid feeding last. But I, for one, do not buy this line of thinking as far as sheepdogs are concerned. There is a lot more to the close relationship and partnership with a sheepdog than the theory that if bossed about they will do what is wanted. Take the wild Dingoes in Australia – probably closer to a border collie dog than a wolf. They hunt in isolation, not in packs, unless the prey is too large for one, in which case they hunt in pairs or small groups and then share the catch. No bossing around there. And nor, in my mind, should there be over-exertion of force and thinking by a handler on a working border collie. By all means take the lead in teaching them what you want them to do, but once they know what is expected, allow them to use their intelligence to arrive at the required outcome. If you have chosen your dog well, trained him in a way that allows him to see what the objective is, and given him the scope to achieve that objective working together with you, then I would say you have a much more valuable dog than one that has been bullied into sitting waiting for its next command.

I have seen handlers try all sorts of different ways to tell a dog they are the boss. Many work on the theory that they should not get too friendly with the dog as this will cause it to lose respect. On the contrary, I always like to get very friendly with my dogs, with the result that they get very close to me and there is a strong bond between the two of us. When giving commands, I like to keep them as quiet as possible. I have found over the years, that if you have a good relationship and handle your dog quietly you will get the best results and the dog is keen to listen. If you have to raise your voice to reprimand them, it is as severe on them as being roughly handled. The closer and kinder you are to your dog, I have found, the better. A raised tone of voice is all that is needed for correction. The dog always knows that if he is getting his commands quietly, then everything is fine and the partnership is working.

Even so, other handlers have different approaches and one of the methods used today, of which I strongly disapprove, is the use of electric collars. These can give the dog a shock at some distance. How would you feel wearing an electric collar? The dogs are not able to concentrate on the job or use their intelligence. They are just waiting for the next shock. Personally I find that you can rely on tone of voice alone if a dog is trained properly from the start. I have always preferred to train my own dogs as some that I have purchased over the years seemed used to being reprimanded.

I once went to see a young dog and was very impressed with him. What I didn't notice at the time though, was that when the owner wanted to call the dog off, he took the sheep into a corner and caught the dog. Liking the dog's way with sheep I decided to buy him and then took him home and let him follow me around for a few days until he got to know me.

One morning when checking over the sheep on the farm, I put him round some sheep and he pleased me well, but when I gave him his call-off command he took off like someone had shot at him. As I had only had him for a few days, I thought I would never see him again. When I came home he was not in the farmyard so, having another dog with me, I went to put him into the kennel which was in a dry, warm loft above the meal house. On the way into the meal house I noticed the new dog crouched underneath a turnip cutter, trembling with fear. I ignored him as I took the dogs up to their kennel but then went into the house and got some meat out of the fridge and took it out to him. He obviously had brains having worked out where to come back to but I had no doubt it was the stick he was expecting, not meat. This was my way of getting through to him that he had done the proper thing in coming back to the barn.

After this I took him out every day and did not ask him to work the sheep at all so that I did not have to call him off. He grew very friendly with me so, after a few weeks, I thought I would risk him around a few sheep at the house. If he bolted again when I called him off he could easily run into the yard. I put him around the sheep and after a few minutes he was really pleasing me, so I got up the courage to give him his call off command. To my surprise he came running back and jumped up on me.

That dog turned out to be one of the best dogs to call off even at long distances and I won a lot of trials with him. I was later to find out when I got his registration card that he had six previous owners but was only two years old.

## A Winning Run

Everyone who enters a sheepdog trial wants to be the one to pick up the trophy. Even if you have no intention of getting involved but happen to find yourself at a trial, it's far more enjoyable if you have some idea of what is going on. Probably the best starting point is to understand where and why points are awarded, and risk being lost, around the course. For those with ambitions to win that trophy, being clear on what the judge is looking for in a good trial run can really help during the early training stages with your dog.

To my mind, a good judge is one with an abundance of common sense, able to draw on their own experience of working with dogs. If in doubt about the decision to make in any situation, a judge should be thinking what would be a practical thing to do in the same situation back at the farm or on the hill. A good judge will also be looking for a trial run with smooth direct lines, the dog taking his sheep where he wants them to go. There is all the difference in the world between this and a dog that just walks after sheep that happen to be going in the right direction. Sheep may not be as herded now as they used to be and as a result are not as good for sheepdog trials, but the right dog can still come out and have a top class run. To achieve that a dog needs to have natural balance and intelligence. Sadly fewer and fewer dogs are allowed to think for themselves or are given the opportunity to use their natural ability. Yet it is still that naturally talented and intelligent dog I am looking for when judging trials and I would hope others are too.

Having worked out what the judge is looking for, the next thing is to try to understand your sheep. Different methods have to be used when handling different types. Hill types such as Swaledale, Scotch Blackface and Cheviot are usually more wild than lowland breeds with the result that the dog has to work quietly around them and stay at a reasonable distance away from them. Lowland breeds such as Mules – Mules being cross-bred Bluefaced Leicester with either Scotch Blackface (Scotch Mule) or Swaledale (North of England Mule) – are much heavier to move, so the dog must work closer and keep the pressure on, not letting them stop. A good dog senses the type of sheep that he is working and adapts himself accordingly.

A mistake that some young handlers make, and some not so young, is that they do not allow for any weak sheep in the batch. Very often, they put on too much pressure with the result that the sheep cannot make the distance.

The most difficult time to work sheep is usually at lambing time when ewes guarding their lambs can sometimes attack the dog. This is a situation when the dog should not give ground by backing off from the sheep in the face of an aggressive attack. Instead it should be prepared to protect itself – but no more than by giving a very aggressive ewe a warning nip on the nose, although this should only be on command and is not allowed at all in trial environments, where, to gain the upper hand, the dog must just stand firm. Some dogs can be too wicked and damage sheep by catching the legs or udders and this I would not tolerate. Weak dogs who run off when the ewe stamps its foot are useless. You can actually manage better without them.

At a trial, one of the first things to do is identify the leading sheep and try to read its movements, keeping one step ahead of it. If you are reading your sheep properly and your timing is spot on, you are probably winning. Think of your dog as a rudder. When steering your boat you do not sit and look at the rudder, you look ahead. It is the same with sheepdog trials. If your dog is properly trained and has natural balance, learn to forget about the dog and watch the leading sheep. If you need only small movements or small flanks to put sheep on line and if the sheep are reacting accordingly, you know things are fine.

And then of course there's the shepherd's whistle – a very important tool to the shepherd and something I've dedicated a lot of time to developing, with some success.

I wouldn't really class myself as an inventor but I do enjoy thinking up ways to make life easier for myself and other farmers or sheepdog handlers. Some early creations have included the 'sheep cradle', a device to keep sheep still and in just the right position to allow for the difficult job of inspecting and treating their feet. That cradle did go into production for a time but was overtaken by events and by companies with better resources to manufacture and market such things than I had access to.

More recently I've had a 'quick hitch' dog lead made up after watching folk struggle to tie up their dogs quickly while they pop off to carry out an errand or pop into a shop. My daughter

Joanne has begun to make and sell those using English Bridle Leather, so we'll see how they do.

Without doubt however, my most successful creations have been my dog whistles.

## Logan Whistles

The whistle is an invaluable tool for a dog handler, allowing him to issue a range of commands that are instantly recognisable to the dog working at long distances – even in terrible weather. A well-trained dog responds instantly to the whistle commands which are easier to regulate than shouting to the dog – which can be confusing or even upsetting if the dog thinks you are displeased rather than just trying to communicate a command.

The basic design of the shepherd's whistle has remained much the same over more years than most of us care to remember. Back in the 1940s nearly all sheepdog whistles were a home-made affair and most handlers had some sort of dubious and probably highly dangerous piece of bent tin in their mouths. In my early years I'd make myself a few whistles from the lids of baked bean tins which weren't the most comfortable of objects to put in your mouth. Through trial and error, I began to produce some that were reasonably effective in creating a sound that the dog could hear a good distance away. I would try them out at sheepdog trials where I could tell if my dogs were able to hear my commands better than was the norm given the course and weather conditions. Back in the 1960s a slightly more sophisticated version was produced by Sammy Holmes and me using metal from the wings of a war-plane that had crashed up in the Mournes. I would say that won me quite a few trials and was invaluable when I was farming the Copeland Islands off County Down in Ireland. But it wasn't until the 1990s that the design really moved on following a chance conversation I had with a retired engineer who had

previously worked in the aircraft industry. I was curious to know how much better a precision-engineered whistle might be and so we set to work.

After considerable thought, investigation and trial, and with the use of a high grade aluminium alloy, we eventually produced what is called the "A1" whistle. The "A1" is very aptly named. Not only is it a top quality whistle, it is "A" shaped and is sculpted from one solid piece of metal, so more hygienic to use than riveted whistles. We have paid particular attention to the acoustic chamber, which is specially contoured to concentrate and project the sound forward, producing a pure, clear tone that can carry over long distances, even in windy, wet or foggy weather. Since the production of the A1, the most original design has probably been a two-holed, brass whistle called the Turbo. This whistle has a lower tone with much more volume, a sound that carries better in windy and misty conditions and one that is very popular with top handlers all over the world. In addition to these, there is also the Supreme, a brass whistle with a sharper tone, the Sterling, made from solid silver and therefore extremely sterile and hygienic, and the gold-plated Jubilee. As I write we are just introducing a stainless steel whistle and one in a new modern non-metallic material, Delrin, which we were attracted to as it is used as an alternative to metal for machined parts that need to remain stable in extreme temperatures – so Formula 1 components, medical equipment…and now Logan Whistles. It should make blowing a Logan Whistle when the temperature is well below freezing a lot more comfortable. All our designs have been tried and tested not only by myself but by my network of friends in the UK, Europe and America – they are popular with many top handlers and used in national and international trials. The multiple tones and commands that can be achieved by the whistles along with their ability to carry sound over long distances and difficult weather conditions mean that they are perfect not only for use with sheepdogs, but also for other dog sports or as a safety or sports whistle. The range is a bestseller at the International Sheepdog Society, and is also sold by my daughter Joanne on her website www.thebordercollie.co.uk. Our whistles are not the only ones around, but they're a locally made product and there are more than a few handlers on the international sheepdog trial stage who will vouch for them being the best.

## Using a sheepdog whistle

A sheepdog whistle is held against the tongue in the mouth and the sound is produced by air flowing through both the holes and out from the 'sound chamber' which is the slit between the two flat sides of the whistle.

If you haven't tried one before, and just like any musical instrument, you will need some practice to be able to produce a range of consistent, controlled sounds. Make sure you are confident in any whistle command before introducing it to a working dog to avoid confusion – or the suggestion that this is a signal for a bit of disobedience. The dog must understand what you mean by each whistle command. To do that, use the whistle tone you want the dog to associate with a specific command and then immediately use the voice command it is already familiar with. After a while you will be able to just use the whistle tone alone allowing you to communicate with the dog at greater distances.

Begin by teaching the dog your most important command – such as a whistle tone which you want the dog to associate with coming back to you. Make sure you use a consistent tone for this command so practise with the whistle out of the dog's hearing until you can produce a clear consistent command.

Here are some tips on how to blow a sheepdog whistle…

1.  Hold the whistle by its tab.
2.  Place the whistle in the mouth so that the tab is to the front and the closed end is against the tongue. Your tongue will be at an angle leaving space below the whistle so as not to block the lower whistle hole.
3.  Hold the whistle in place with the lips – they seal the edges of the whistle so that air can only escape through the slit at the front. You can use your hand to push the back of the whistle against your tongue so that air in the mouth goes through the holes and out the slit at the front. Play with the placement of the whistle against the tongue – some people push it against the tip of their tongue, others a little further back and some under their tongue! The key is to find a place that is most comfortable, allows your lips to fall easily around the front (without blocking the slit) and that keeps the whistle holes clear while you blow through the whistle.
4.  Breathe out hard through your mouth with air all around the whistle so that air is pushed through BOTH the small circular holes inside your mouth, and leaves between the slit formed by the top and bottom of the whistle.
5.  Your tongue on the back of the whistle will vary the direction of the air, and after a little trial and error, you will soon master the art.

| COMMAND | WHAT IT SOUNDS LIKE | WHAT THE DOG SHOULD DO |
|---|---|---|
| Lie down | One high pitch blast - not too long | Lie down |
| Get up & walk on (Walk Up) | Series of short whistles (start with 2 short 'wheeps' - more if needed) | Stand and walk straight towards livestock. If you want the dog to move faster repeat the whistles faster & louder |
| 'Come Bye' (Left Flank) | Chew-or-ee - full left flank<br>Chew - short left flank<br>(first note like a bird's chirp) | Go Clockwise - arc around the LEFT side of the sheep - a full long flank is the movement of the dog round the sheep - almost the whole left side of the sheep. If you want to completely circle the sheep repeat the full-long flank command until the dog comes right round.<br><br>Using the first 'chirp' note of the command, 'Chew' is a 'half-flank' which tells the dog to move just a short distance around the left side of the sheep. |
| Away Here (Right flank) | Wha-Heee - full right flank<br>Wha - half right flank | Go anti-clockwise - i.e. arc around the RIGHT side of the sheep |
| Take Time | He-He<br>Short blast repeated only if necessary | Slows dog to a steady pace |
| Look Back | Who-Hee-Who-Hee<br>or<br>Whe-Whee-oo<br>(the well known 'wolf whistle') | Turns dog around to go gather more livestock |
| Call Off - 'That'll do' | Wheet-ew-Wheet<br>or<br>Whee-ew-Whee-ew | Orders dog to stop working & return to handler |

There are a number of commands that are commonly used for working sheepdogs, with a few variations and these are described in the table on the previous page. You can though create your own commands. The key is to make sure that each command is very different so the dog is able to distinguish between them easily.

## A Special Time and Some Special Wins

I recently joined in the celebrations and judged the fiftieth anniversary of a sheepdog trial in Dromara, County Down which was, as it turns out, also a fiftieth anniversary for me – I had won the very first trial there all those years ago. When I look back, and only considering the wins I had in Single competitions, I can count that I've won seven National competitions, six for Ireland and one for Scotland, represented Ireland at International level at least twenty-two times, Scotland on another three occasions and been in the Supreme Championship, the top fifteen handlers in the country, on seven occasions over the years.

It was, though, moving to Scotland in the early 'eighties and having the pleasure of running under some of the old-time handlers and judges there, that I really believe was the making of me not only as a sheepdog handler, but also as a trial judge. I learned a lot about handling dogs and judging trials in conversation with these very practical men who owed their livelihood to working with sheep and dogs.

Later I took that experience with me when I began to judge sheepdog trials and take clinics in North America – but more of that later. First a few stories about those wins and the dogs that made it happen.

After my success with Nell in 1967, my first all-Ireland National win came in 1968 at Tallaght outside Dublin with a two-year old dog, Moy. I had bought her when she was ten months old from David Brady and her sire was Jimmy Brady's Buff, himself an Irish National winner. Moy was only a year and eleven months on the day she won the competition. She had been sixth the previous year at eleven months' old and I was very proud of her. She was a very promising young bitch with a great future. But that future was taken away when the vet at the National, Doctor Barnett, found evidence of the eye condition PRA – progressive retinal atrophy. This is a hereditary eye disorder in dogs which can eventually lead to blindness, but which is detectable and it is something the International Sheepdog Society was taking serious steps to try to eradicate in the border collie breed. Any dog over the age of two being entered for a National sheepdog competition must have a clear ophthalmic certificate, and any dogs showing the disease cannot be used for breeding. As Moy was not quite two when Dr Barnett examined her, I was advised to take her to a Mr Grimes in Dublin who was the only person in Ireland at that time who could carry out an official eye-test. It was frustrating to have such a talented dog's future taken away, but in the fight to stem the occurrence of PRA in border collies, it was a price dog handlers increasingly had to pay.

The loss of Moy was made up for the following year when I won the Irish National with Cap, this time in Castlewellan, a town nestled in the Mournes near the holiday resort of Newcastle. Cap had been through quite a few handlers by the time he came to me and it was generally thought that he would not make the grade. It meant that I was able to buy him for 'handy money' in the autumn of 1967. By the following May he competed in, and won, his first trial at the Dublin Spring Show. Not only did he win the National in 1969, but he also went on to be in the Irish team at the International five times, competing in both the Singles and the Brace. If that Irish National Trophy could talk, it might have a few stories to tell about me. On the way home from the 1969 National in Castlewellan, a water hose in the car burst and I had to tie it up as best I could with a handkerchief. This meant that the radiator had to be topped up fairly often, and as the only water-carrying device I had at my disposal was the National Trophy, it was unceremoniously dunked in any cattle drinking trough or stream I came upon on the way home. It was to be filled with stronger liquor on later occasions.

In July 1974 at Fermoy, County Cork, and then again in 1977 at Ashford, County Wicklow, I won the Irish National with a dog called Jim bought from a well respected sheepdog handler, Peter Hetherington. Jim had also been through a lot of handlers before he got to Peter's. He was originally sold to a handler in Scotland, then to a third in Wales, and back again to a fourth in Scotland before I eventually bought him and brought him to Ireland. I'd seen him run when I was at Peter's place and just liked him. He seemed to me to have a lot of natural style and talent. With me, Jim qualified to run in five Irish Nationals, (winning twice) and qualified for the Irish team at the International Championship five times in succession. He also won the Irish Brace Championship in 1975 and was Irish Driving Champion in 1976. In 1978 he came sixth in the Supreme Championship (a competition between the best fifteen dogs from the four nations) at the International in Chatsworth.

After any National competition, there is always a bit of celebrating to do, such as the dance that was held in 1974 at Fermoy. As the winner, I asked the bar-man if he could sell me a bottle to fill the cup to share with the other competitors. I expected him to fill it with whiskey which was the custom at that time and I'm sure there was some whiskey in there, but that wasn't all. I took one sip before it was passed around and that was enough. It would have taken paint off a barn door. On its way around I saw one gentleman in our party taking quite a few sips. When the dance band finished and we were heading to our beds in the hotel, this particular gentleman was missing. Although we noticed, we didn't think too much of it for he was a very eligible bachelor and maybe he had got a girlfriend. By the next morning it was clear that his bed had not been slept in and we were just beginning to get a little bit anxious about him, when someone happened to visit a downstairs toilet and found him fast asleep on the bowl. Not usually a man to be found in such an embarrassing position he maintained he was not suffering for the enthusiasm he'd shown for the sharing cup. It was, he said, a case of having been poisoned by the silver polish. The cup was, apparently, full of it. We didn't argue. And who knows, he might have been right. None of us had got as closely acquainted with it as he had.

At Jim's second National win in 1977 at Ashford, quite a few of us were staying in the same digs and would go out each evening for a meal, getting back quite late. All except the two chaps that I was travelling with who, being teetotal, preferred to stay in the hotel and go to bed early. When I came back one evening I spied in the hall area of the guest house a lifesize figure of a lady. Being in quite good spirits I decided to pick up this figurine and take it to the room of my slumbering companions. There I slipped her in beside the chap who had claimed the double bed and covered her up with his blanket. When I came down the next morning for breakfast, my two friends were sitting at the table. As usual, they had been up in good time. I says to this chap, 'Is your lady friend not coming down for breakfast?' 'No,' he says to me under his breath, 'she has a headache.' I've always wondered what the chamber maid thought when she found that lady in the bed.

Two years later, in 1980 I won the Irish National with Sweep at the famous Curragh Race Course in County Kildare, the scene of the Irish Derby. I was the second dog to run on the last day of the trial and I knew that Sweep had put up a run, one that would be very hard to beat. The sheep weren't all that good, but when the going was difficult and the sheep were hard to handle, that's when Sweep was at his best. He seemed to be able to mesmerise these wild unruly sheep. And he made a first class job of it. So I relaxed for most of the day with a chap from County Wicklow, Pat Malloy. We spent the day up in the grandstand and had a fine view of the trial unfurl and, as they say in Ireland, the craic was good.

After I'd won and been presented with the cup, I invited everyone around me that I knew up to the lounge in the grandstand. As was the tradition, I was going to fill the cup. I had arranged this with the bar man who told me that, instead of the whiskey we'd normally use, they had special champagne that they used at race meetings. He said he'd fill the cup at a good price. Well, I thought, it would be something new for the old cup.

So all my friends started to come up to the bar, bringing their dogs with them. Jimmy Brady was second that day and his son David was third – both Jimmy and David are top class handlers. There was a great atmosphere and, as everyone was gathered around, I popped the cork on the champagne to fill the cup. At the sound of the cork popping, Jim Brady's bitch bolted out the door, down the steps of the grandstand and across the racecourse with Jimmy hightailing it after her to try to get her calmed down. The last words I heard Jimmy uttering as he headed to the steps were, 'God curse you, Logan, and your bloody fancy champagne.'

I'd bought Sweep in Scotland when he was nine months old, the grandson of the famous Winston Cap – the dog used for the logo of the International Sheepdog Society. Sweep went on to become International Driving Champion and qualify for the Supreme Championship at the International in the same year at Ballagh in Wales. This was just at a time when I sold the farm in Ireland and moved to a hill farm, Lagnaha, near Fortwilliam in the West Highlands of Scotland. In 1981 Sweep and I switched allegiance and represented the Scottish National Team at the International where he got through to the Supreme Championship again, this time at Armouthwaite, which is between Carlisle and Penrith. Sweep was probably one of the most consistent trial winners I had, having won twenty-four Open Trials by the time he was only four and half years old.

In 1981 it was Star's turn to win a National, this time the Scottish National at Glamis Castle. He too went on to represent Scotland at Supreme Championship level at Blair Athyll, Penrithshire. I had bought Star as a six-month-old pup from David Gibson in Scotland. He was very good from a very young age, winning his first open trial over a six-hundred-yard Outrun when he was only eleven months old. After this trial was all over, a world-renowned handler, Tom Watson, one of the best handlers that Scotland has produced, came to me and shook my hand and congratulated me. He says to me, 'Harford, what have you done to us? This is the first time the Scottish team will be going down to England to the International with an Irish captain.'

These dogs are all tough acts to follow but my next notable Singles trial successes were with what I consider to be one of my very best dogs, Dick. Dick was bred and trained in the second farm we worked in Scotland, Well House in Wigtownshire. His father was Mickey (he had been part of the Brace Team I had won the One Man and his Dog competition with in 1988) and his mother was Jean, Jean being a grand-daughter of one of my best dogs, Sweep. Dick did not run in the National until he was over three years old but soon made up for lost time. Whilst he never won the National, he qualified five times in succession for the Irish team between 1992 and 1996, qualifying three times for the Supreme Championship and coming fourth, fifth and ninth on each attempt. He also won the Northern Ireland Sheepdog Society Trial over an International style course in 1994.

*Dick's father at work.*

# TRAINING A CHAMPION

## Choices, Choices

When I am asked advice on training a dog, my mind always goes back to Dick, one of my most successful dogs. All dogs are different and before you launch into training you need to have taken time to figure out their unique temperament, natural abilities and weaknesses. You then need to tailor training to suit the dog, keep it interested and keep it learning at the right pace. Everyone runs into different problems when training dogs. It's advisable when a problem comes up not to be too hasty in trying to fix it, but over some time try to find the problem from the dog's point of view. If this can be figured out, it is much more easily solved and well worth the extra time spent on it.

I trained Dick from a puppy to become one of the most successful working and trial sheepdogs of his generation – and the following is my account of how we achieved that together. That is not to say that this is the right or only way to train a sheepdog, but it certainly worked well for me with the boisterous, headstrong puppy, Dick.

Dick was born at Wellhouse Farm – our second farm in Scotland. By then my children had all grown up and left home, so when he was around eight weeks old I took him and another puppy to Joe McLaughlin who lived in Saintfield, County Down. The deal was for him to rear the two puppies until they were eight months old and in return he could keep the one I chose not to train.

In my view, it is very important for a puppy to get lots of freedom, to be able to explore and see what is going on around the farmyard. Many folk are training young dogs as a business. They keep too many and it is more or less a puppy factory with the result they do not get enough individual attention or the chance to socialise with folk. Being exposed to kindness and learning their name makes all the difference and lays a good foundation for later on when training is started.

Joe was semi-retired and looked after sheep for a neighbour. He was a butcher by trade and still worked a few hours when required. The result was that the puppies were very well fed with butcher scraps and Joe's grandchildren walked them around on the lead and played with them.

When the puppies were six months' old, they started to sneak out of the yard to the sheep in the nearby field. This was giving Joe trouble with the result that he rang me to ask if I could come and collect one of the puppies. I took my pick and Joe got the other one for his trouble, as we had agreed. One was 'showing eye' as we say and was very classy and the other one was just a boisterous puppy. Although that boisterous pup was a bit of a handful, I could see flashes in him that I liked so this was the one that I decided to take. The other one was just too nice for its age. Joe was fairly surprised but relieved that it was the boisterous puppy I chose that day. 'I was kinda hoping you'd take that one,' he said. 'He's a bit of a handful for me.'

Dick matured very quickly and once ready for trialling, he came second in the Scottish Nursery Finals and two weeks later won his first Open Trial amongst strong opposition. His son Cap almost bettered him. He won the Irish Nursery Final and came second in his first Open – which he should have won if I had been able to overcome my knee problem and give him more help at the Shed.

# Early Training

I t was only once I brought the puppy back home that I called him Dick. Then, when he was about eight months' old, I decided to give him some light training as he was getting out of control.

It is always a handler's dream to find a puppy showing natural talent and the most important thing during early training is not to knock that natural talent out of the dog. Too much training creates robots. My preference is not to train dogs like soldiers so they do what they are told and nothing else. Let the dog use its natural talent and its brain and trust it to learn to think for itself. In work situations on the hill, a dog that can think for itself when out of the handler's sight is worth its weight in gold.

A lot of things in early training do not make much sense to a puppy, such as to lie down, stand, stay and come to the handler when called, but as time goes on they fall into place. You can begin to train a puppy in all of these commands at an early stage, well before the puppy is taken to sheep. This then gives the handler some control when the puppy is introduced to stock and makes life a lot simpler later on in training. Early training can be done in spare time, or in some cases in the house at night. This is an important stage in building an understanding between puppy and handler, helped by the fact that the puppy does not have the distraction of stock to take its mind off the task in hand.

Dick already knew how to walk on the lead so I gave him some basic training – to lie down, stand up and come to me when called. In the first few lessons I pushed him down to the ground and told him to lie down, then got him on his feet and made him stand still until I walked away a few paces. I then asked him to come to me and praised him when he did. He was then ready to be introduced to a few sheep in a small paddock for his initial training.

By now I had been able to study Dick and could tell what

his natural traits were. I was beginning to decide the type of approach that I would need to take to train him – they are all individual.

With Dick, it took a few lessons on the sheep before he would listen well enough to stop and then to come away from the sheep on the 'call off' signal. With a dog with his enthusiasm I knew this was to be expected and didn't let it affect the tone I used giving him his commands.

Dick was quite boisterous as a puppy and being so keen, he liked to get his own way. With my knee problems it was often difficult to be in the right place at the right time to correct him so I had to find a way to counteract his enthusiasm. An older dog I had at the time, Mickey, kept things under control, as he was happy to stay in one place until things were getting difficult for the young dog.

If Dick got a chance at all, he would like to be in amongst the sheep and, with me being slow, this was a problem. I even thought I might have to get someone to start this tough young dog as I was not getting between him and the sheep fast enough. But then I had the idea of driving a paling post into the middle of the paddock and tying a sheep to it. With the sheep confined to the post it was easy to keep Dick off as the sheep was more or less stationary. He did try a few times to get in and get a grip of the sheep but now I was able to stop him. As I did I would say, 'What do you think you are doing?' in a stern voice and he quickly got to know when he heard these words that I was not pleased with him and he kept back off the sheep.

At the end of each lesson I would move clockwise round the sheep and give him his 'come bye' command at the same time. I would do this a few times in a clockwise direction, stopping him about twice on every circuit to stop him going into orbit. Then I reversed the procedure so he was taking the sheep anti-clockwise and then I'd give him the 'away here' command. He was sure of commands for each side after about two or three days. I reckon that simple paling post and one sheep had achieved three things. It had solved my mobility problem, it kept the sheep from being abused by a boisterous young dog and it was a very quick way to teach Dick the commands for both sides.

After this I let five or six sheep into the paddock and got Mickey to hold them in the centre. I took Dick within fifteen yards of the sheep and made him stop and stay until I got close up to the sheep. Then I gave him a flank command and if he came up too close towards the sheep I said to him, 'What do you think you are doing?' Remembering his lesson with the stationary sheep, he gave them plenty of room. I increased the distance by about five yards each day and kept myself further from the sheep as well. It was not very long before he developed a nice cast round the sheep and I could send him away from beside my foot.

I always ask my dogs to stand when setting them up for sheep and they quickly know to look for sheep when they hear the word 'Stand'. If they are impatient and want to break away for the sheep before being told, I would take them back and put them in their kennels. I would then take them out three or four times a day and tell them to Stand and then put them back in their kennels. I have found this a good method for stopping dogs breaking away before they have been told to.

The most unnatural thing for a dog is taking sheep away from the handler. Instead they instinctively want to bring the sheep to you. In a trial situation a dog's ability to take sheep away from the handler is tested in what's called the Drive section of the course. Dick was to come to that stage much later in his training. In the early stages young dogs should be asked to do simple things and until further into their training should not be asked to accomplish any task that the handler knows would be difficult for them to complete – in other words a young dog should be asked to do only what he is mature enough to understand. Have enough patience to keep the early training simple.

# The Silent Gather

One of the very first practical things you need a sheepdog to do on command is to run out into the field or up the hill, and without scattering or spooking the sheep, bring them to you at a steady pace. As the dog gets more experienced it will more often than not have to bring the sheep through a series of openings in the hedges or stone walls. This is a basic skill and is the first task a dog and handler are challenged with in a sheepdog trial. The whole movement is called the 'Gather', and involves three key stages:

*The Outrun* (20 points) – the action of the dog running out around and behind the sheep, ideally without them seeing him.

*The Lift* (10 points) – the first movement of the sheep under the control of the dog.

*The Fetch* (20 points) – the movement of the sheep down the course to the handler through a set of gates on the way to simulate the obstacles the dog may find in a real working environment.

At the start of most sheepdog trials the sheep are three or four hundred yards away from the handler and dog. In International Competitions the distance will be about half a mile – more akin to the type of distance an experienced dog would have to run to pick up sheep in a working environment on hills. My fully trained dogs worked as far away as a mile from me in the hills and glens of Lagnaha. The whistle would not travel that distance on a windy day and so, once out of ear-shot, I would have to rely on them to use their own intelligence to work the sheep. To have a dog you can depend on to do that, you need one that has been trained in such a way that he understands *why* he is doing something, not just responding to commands automatically.

When I am judging how a dog runs out to pick up the sheep I am looking for one that runs away from the handler in a nice wide arc, reaching the widest point when level with the sheep and then going around behind them at a nice distance. The shape of this movement up, round and then behind the sheep is often referred to as a 'pear-shaped Outrun'. I do not mind the dog hitting the fence during his Outrun providing he does not then use it as a guide towards the sheep. It's therefore important when teaching Outruns to a young dog, to make sure it can see the sheep and so understand the task, rather than just train them to move on command out to the fence. A dog looking for sheep rather than a fence is naturally, in the long run, a more sensible Outrunner, especially on open ground.

It doesn't matter if the dog runs up the left or right side in a trial environment. That's down to the handler and what he thinks is best on the occasion. Sometimes you find a dog that has a preferred side – always tending to run up and then behind the sheep from either the left or the right. To avoid this, I trained Dick to work from both ends of the field so that he got used to the pressure from both sides. Sheep are inclined to head one way in a field and put pressure on one side and if a young dog gets accustomed to pressure on one side it can end up a one-sided dog.

A 'one-sided' dog can actually be a real danger in a working environment. When I was working Lagnaha, our hill farm in the Western Scottish Highlands, sheep would very often be very close to the edge of a gully. Even if there was only a small space on the gully side, I would have to send the dog up on that side. If the dog had come up from the other side, where there was more space, the sheep may well have panicked and run towards the gully, maybe even jumped in.

While I'm on the subject, 'Crossed Outruns' are a very serious mistake. By that I mean that the dog heads off on one side to pick up the sheep but then changes his mind and crosses over the course in front of the sheep, rather than sneaking up behind them unseen. In working situations the sheep would see the dog and most likely bolt before it has a chance to get behind them.

If a dog slows up too much at the end of his Outrun, it is more or less the same as stopping altogether. The outcome in everyday work would be that the dog would lose its sheep. Sheep can get away very quickly on their own ground and a dog needs to run well into the head of them to stop them.

The Lift refers to the action by the dog to get the sheep moving off the point where they have been grazing and is the point at which the dog takes control. At this important stage, I like to see a dog stopping well behind his sheep on what is called the 'point of balance', and then walking directly up to them at a steady pace, not to excite them or spook them. It's much the same principle as letting a clutch out in a car. If you let the clutch out nice and gently, you'll start off gently. If you let a clutch out with a bang, the car will probably take a couple of buck leaps which wouldn't be too comfortable for the passengers. The same with sheep. They would probably take fright and take off at forty miles an hour. If there were heavily pregnant ewes they might even abort some of the lambs. Or if they were in the middle of lambing there may be some weak lambs to contend with. So that's why the combination of the Outrun and the Lift is the main part of a winning run at a trial. If you start them off wrong at the top, you never get them settled again.

Once the dog has run around the sheep, ideally without them knowing, turned up unannounced behind where they stand, at or near the Post, and then 'Lifted' them by getting them moving as a group, the next task is to bring them in a controlled way and at a nice steady pace down the course towards the handler, through a set of gates on the way. This is referred to as the Fetch and to be good, the sheep should have a smooth journey in a straight line directly to the handler. The sheep should not stop until they come to the bottom of the course – a sign that they are being driven by a good, balanced dog. Some handlers let their sheep stop as they come into the Fetch gates but the chances are that they will 'spook' when they are moved again and be more likely to miss the obstacle.

If the sheep are veering off slightly, the dog should be allowed to use its own initiative to move out on to the pressure to keep the sheep in a straight line, putting in nice short balanced movements to keep a steady flowing run. This is what is called a short flank and if given at the proper time saves the need for a bigger correction when it is too late – the old saying 'a stitch in time saves nine'. Over-flanking causes sheep to go off line with a large loss of points at a trial.

Whenever Dick was learning the Gather, I would stop him behind the sheep at the point of balance and tell him to 'walk up'. Then I would walk backwards in front of the sheep. If the sheep were getting out of position I would move myself to keep the line straight. I think it is important to keep young dogs in a direct line behind the sheep. I did this for a week, gradually staying further back off the sheep myself.

When he was ten months old Dick was capable of running out two hundred yards and, because he had noticed during his initial training I wanted the lines kept straight, he gradually started to balance himself to do just that. I would occasionally put him out to the sheep at this age, stop him behind them, then tell him to 'get up' but give no more commands until the sheep were brought to me. This developed his balance and his pace, two very important skills in a working dog and something we seem to be losing in the modern dogs.

Because Dick was given time during his training to understand what was being asked of him, he became a much more useful working dog. He was also a life saver at trials. On one occasion when competing with Dick, I dropped my whistle in the long grass just as he left my foot. By the time I found it he was coming though the Fetch gates with the sheep. That's what I mean by natural ability and control and that's why I was impressed, when judging in America, with what they called a 'Silent Gather' for breaking ties in a trial.

On the Silent Gather the dog was sent out to collect the sheep and no commands were allowed to be given until the sheep were back at the handler's feet, each command given being a loss of points. This identified the naturally balanced dogs that could be sent out to do a job out of sight. This is something which I think should be encouraged. It is always interesting to see what is in a dog when it is left to its own devices.

At the beginning of his training Dick did not want to leave the sheep. I taught him by tying twenty yards of twine to his collar and when I told him, 'That will do,' I made sure I had hold of the twine to teach him to come away with me. He soon got the message and I would praise him for coming back to me. It is most important to have a good hold of the cord before saying, 'That will do.'

## Learning to Drive

After the Outrun, Lift and Fetch were perfected, I then began to teach Dick to drive his sheep with confidence where he wanted them to go. If the Lift was the equivalent to letting out the clutch in a car, then the Drive is all about selecting the right gear. You need a dog to have a low gear and a few faster gears. When a dog is walking and you don't want him to stop you need to select a low gear, so you tell him to 'take time'. You can then move up the gears by giving a series of whistles – the louder and more urgent the whistle, the faster the dog will go. If you want sheep turned in a hurry, then you can give the flank command fairly loudly and he will move on to the pressure at top speed. This is the over-drive. The steering is the ability you have to put the dog left or right on command. Once a dog learns his right and left commands, he always acts on the command instantly – there never seems to be any confusion as there can easily be when you ask humans to go right or left. Instead the reaction seems to become instinctive with a dog. When I give a stop command

I like to see a dog stop instantly on its feet – just like applying the brakes in a car in an emergency stop.

The Drive is a task that dogs have to perform quite often during a working day, maybe shifting a flock of sheep to new pastures. The dog stays behind the sheep and keeps driving them in front of the shepherd. There used to be a lot of driving on roads but now it's nearly impossible with so much traffic. In Lagnaha in Scotland I often had to drive the sheep along the forestry roads on the mountains – over a mile of good safe tracks to guide the sheep along towards the farm. These roads were very seldom disturbed by traffic, but if the sheep did happen to take a sudden dive up into the trees, I would give the dog his right or left hand command as needed to get them rounded up and then bring him back behind the sheep again.

My focus was therefore to teach Dick to move in smooth direct lines at a good steady pace behind his sheep. The sheep should not be given the chance to stop – sheep standing still are not being driven.

In a trial environment a dog's control over sheep is tested in the Drive section of the course (*30 points; 40 at World Championships*) which involves taking the sheep in straight lines around a three-sided triangle, each side being around 150 yards long, and negotiating two sets of gates on the way.

To begin to teach the Drive with a young dog, you should always make sure you have free-moving sheep that will move off easily. I not only made sure Dick was behind the sheep, but I also stayed alongside him to keep him walking in a straight line. If he was getting out of position to one side, I did not try and flank him back into position. Instead I went across between him and the sheep on to his other side, leaving him behind the sheep again. I kept him walking after his sheep and even if I got only a few yards at a time, as soon as I noticed him getting out of position, I stopped him immediately and reversed my position to his other side before carrying on again.

Even though by this stage he knew the commands for each

side, I preferred to teach him the Drive in this way, rather than give him 'flank' commands to move him from side to side as he drove the sheep. I have found over the years that giving a young dog flank commands on his drive can break his concentration with the result that you can have them looking back at you. A mistake that is often made is using the 'call off' to get them into position. It is my opinion that a dog should only be called off when asked to come right back to the handler.

I never use flanks on the Drive with a young dog until they can drive their sheep for around fifty or sixty yards using only their 'Walk up' command. The first dog I used this method on was Sweep back in the early 'seventies and he went on to win the International Driving championship at Balla, Wales.

After each training session, I would finish off by putting Dick round the sheep twice on his 'come bye' side – stopping him twice each time round to keep him from just running automatically without thinking of the command – and then repeating on the 'away here' side. He was then ready to be introduced gradually to the flank commands on both Fetch and Drive.

Because Dick was taught to keep his lines straight on both Fetch and Drive, he did not need a lot of flanking on either. The only thing that he needed now was work experience and to be taught to 'up' or 'slow down' his pace on command.

## The Pen

Not all the jobs you need a dog to help you with are out in the open. Very often you need a dog to help you gather sheep into an enclosed space in readiness for shearing or dipping. And every year you need to load sheep onto the lorry to go to market. One of my most memorable dogs, Jim, regularly had the task of loading sheep on and off a fishing boat. This was maybe a bit out of the ordinary, but still called on the same basics skills of balance and control. It certainly wouldn't be much use if you succeeded in rounding up sheep on a mountain and getting them safely back to the farm if you couldn't then get them into a pen.

So this is another phase in the trial which is needed in everyday work – the Pen (10 points), often the most photographed and so most-recognised phase. This is a small fenced-in enclosure with a gate which can be closed once the sheep are safely inside. At the Pen stage of a trial, or in any situation where the same close management of stock is needed, I like to see a dog on his feet balancing his sheep and taking control of them. If you watch really good Penning in a sheepdog trial, the dog seems to move very little, but can hold the sheep with balance and eye contact. Just a step to one side or a sway of their body is enough to correct a movement. If a

dog can do this on his own, he is in a position to see the need for corrections much earlier than the handler and so can make the right movement at the right time. Many dogs I see at the Pen have been expertly obedience trained and so do only as they are told. That means they respond to their handler's call – which is usually too late or too soon – and do not put in that wee movement of their own which would most likely have been spot on.

I remember being at trials in Kilmacolm in Scotland when at two o'clock in the afternoon no one had managed to get a single sheep in the Pen. They were almost impossible. Bob Shennan came out with old Mirk who was about twelve years old at that time and probably at his last trial. Though I am not a betting man, I said to the folk standing around that I would wager anyone a pound that Mirk would Pen the sheep. No one took me on but when Mirk brought them to the mouth of the Pen he hardly moved. He swayed his body, took the odd step to the side and before we knew it, the sheep were Penned. Old Mirk had managed to put the first sheep in the Pen that day after maybe twenty or thirty runs.

When Penning wild, touchy sheep it is very important when you get them stopped in front of the Pen to let them settle, and very often when they settle for a short time, one will lead them into the Pen. This is usually the case with Blackface ewe lambs. This is a place where much haste makes less speed.

With old Mirk in mind, I allowed Dick to use his own natural instinct to read the sheep at close range and gave him plenty of practice so he could work out his own way of controlling the situation.

## What's this Shedding all About?

After getting some work experience, I introduced Dick to Shedding.

In everyday working, the Shed is used for tasks such as manoeuvring lame or otherwise distressed sheep away from the rest of the flock. This avoids having to take the whole flock in to ensure treatment of a few. Sometimes a single sheep needs to be taken off. This might be a ewe having difficulty lambing which you then need the dog to cut off from the rest of the flock and bring close enough to you so you can put your shepherd's crook round her neck or leg to catch her and give her assistance in delivery of the lamb. Anyone who is familiar with 'cowboying' will have seen the cowboys cut off a single cow or a few they need. This is exactly the same principle as the Shed in a sheepdog trial except the cowboy separates the cow with a specially bred horse for the job called a Cutting Horse. Apparently Cutting Horse competitions are big business in North America.

In a trial the Shed and Single is the final part of the course and is a test of how well the dog can hold the sheep in one spot. In the National and International qualifying rounds where there are only five sheep, two are marked with ribbons or collars. In the first Shed you have to separate off two of the three unmarked sheep from the group of five. In the second Shed or 'Single' you then have to separate one of the two marked sheep. In the Supreme Championship and World Trials five ribboned sheep have to be shed from the twenty. Each Shed attracts a maximum of ten points.

When I was teaching Dick to Shed, I started with a fairly large batch of sheep. I would let the sheep run past me, with the dog on the opposite side, and would then ask the dog to come in as the sheep were running, not worrying where he came in or how he came in just as long as he came flying in to stop them. The running sheep gave the task a matter of urgency for the dog and so it was more effective than using stationary sheep. After this stage I would make an opening for him to come in and then turned him to the sheep that I wanted to drive off. This was always his last task of the day, so I would ask him to drive the sheep off to the gate to give him some purpose in what he was doing. After a few weeks when coming in on the Shed, he knew he had to take control and drive them off. When he was Shedding perfectly on the larger batch of sheep, I then introduced him to shedding six or eight sheep. After a few lessons on the smaller batch of sheep I then taught him to take a Single by stopping the last sheep.

A single sheep tests a dog more than any other work and it is something which I do not think we have enough of in trials nowadays. Taking a single sheep was one thing that Dick found difficult at the beginning. He was good at coming in on a split: for this his command was 'Here, Dick' and for the last sheep it was 'This Yin'. I thought, 'How can I make this single

sheep easy for him?' and in the end decided to put a langle on one sheep. Many people will not now know what a langle is, but these are made out of plaited stack rope with a loop on either end. This was attached to the hind leg and the front leg and was widely used in old style farming when sheep wire was not available and fences were not good. When the sheep were brought down from the hills at lambing time, they would be langled on the same side and changed to the other side weekly to keep their legs from being damaged.

When I put the langle on one sheep in the batch, she could not move as fast as the other sheep and as she was walking in a different way from the rest of the sheep, it was easy to draw Dick's attention to her. So when I said, 'This Yin,' he soon got quite keen on this last sheep, mainly because of its strange movement. I would take the langle off the sheep after each lesson, but I always put it back on the same sheep for the next lesson. This meant that after a few days she was almost able to keep up with the other sheep, therefore making the job of taking the Single more difficult day by day. After about a week or ten days, I introduced Dick to taking the Single without the sheep being langled and in a short time he was Singling perfectly.

When judging sheepdog trials I find fault with many handlers going in and splitting sheep themselves, then calling in their dog. Worse still, quite a few walk along with their dog assisting them to drive the sheep off. A Shed such as that deserves, at most, one point. The dog should demonstrate that it is in full control of the sheep and has shed off the two or single sheep required, not just taken the easy option of turning on to sheep that are already running away.

I have often thought that we could reward the best dogs at the Shed if there were no ribbons on the sheep. When there are marked sheep, the handler and dog can wait until they become separate from the rest or move to the front of the group and become easy pickings. This suits weak shedding dogs. Far better in my view, to leave them all unmarked and simply ask the handler to hold back the last one or two rather than pick off the sheep which are more or less shedding themselves.

At Supreme Championship or World Trial level, I would consider changing the task in the Shedding ring which at the moment, requires five marked sheep to be Shed from a flock of twenty. Many people agree that more luck is attached to the Shedding than any other section of the course. Yet winning many Internationals can hinge on the Shedding in the Final.

On one occasion in the Supreme Championship at Bala with Sweep, I did not complete because of one difficult sheep. Afterwards someone comments, 'It's a pity he's not a better shedder.' But I knew that was not the case as was proven a year later at Amerathwaite when two of the judges gave him full points at the Supreme Shed and the other took only one point off.

At the Seaforde International trial in 2002 only two competitors completed the Shed. Even Stuart Davidson did not have time to pen the sheep after the Shed in his winning run. In the Mostyn International Supreme final with one of my very best dogs, Dick, I had a lead of seventeen points coming into the Shedding Ring but due to a difficult last sheep and my own mobility problem (knees that have been up a few too many hills), I was unable to complete. Dick was actually a good shedder as he proved when completing the Supreme course at Aberystwyth. When judging the American Final in Oklahoma some years ago, only the winning dog completed the Shedding, but again, he did not have time to complete the run. In fact in 2003 no one in the American Finals got the Shed completed, not even the winner.

Maybe we could test the shedding ability of the dog in the Supreme Championship by following the same principle as that used in the National and Qualifying rounds. In other words, be required to take some of the marked sheep out of the group, but not all. Instead of taking five ribboned sheep off the group of twenty, reduce the stress for the dog and the sheep by increasing the number of ribboned sheep in the group of twenty to say six or seven and then shedding five from these. I say this because very often the fifth and last ribboned sheep to be peeled away from the group is very reluctant to leave. This might be because it was targeted earlier and so resorts to burying itself in the group out of the way. At the same time, given that the Shed may by now have gone on for some time, you will probably have to deal with sheep that are trying to escape. Trying to deal at the same time with one sheep that is burying itself into the middle and another that is intent on bolting is almost impossible when you only have one dog.

Another suggestion might be something along the lines of an interesting Shed which I have done at Demonstrations using ten sheep. I split five and five, holding the last five and letting them away one by one until a single sheep is left. There is not so much luck attached to this and a good shedding dog is required.

# Whistle While You Work

At about this point in Dick's training I began to change from voice to whistle commands. When you do this it is very important to have different tones for right and left commands, especially for the first part of each whistle. When a dog is working properly on whistles, it is the first part of each command that he acts on.

When changing a dog to whistle commands I have always given the whistle command for the appropriate side first, followed by the voice command. Many trainers do this the opposite way, that is, voice command followed by the whistle. I have found that the former works better for me and dogs change easily as they soon come to associate the whistle as the first part of the appropriate voice command. Using this system, most dogs will change in around a week to ten days.

When running brace competitions I always had my dogs trained so that when I called a dog by name, the other dog immediately stopped. The way I went about doing this, for instance when working Jim and Sweep, was as follows. I would command Jim to Walk Up by calling, 'Jim Jim,' and almost immediately after this I would say, 'Sweep, Lie Down.' It wasn't long before the penny dropped and when one dog heard the other's name he knew he was about to get his Lie Down command, each soon realising that hearing the other's name was his command to stop. When I wanted the two dogs to move together, they would do so on the same Walk Up whistle. The same applied when doing demonstrations with four or five dogs. The only command they had in common was the Walk Up whistle. This works no matter how many dogs are on the team and certainly made life a lot easier for me. Doubles team dogs have to be well matched – you don't want one dog forcing on and the other having to be coaxed on – both must be equally balanced. I find that two good line dogs are much better for doubles work than wide running dogs, as they will follow their sheep and keep them in line. I had several tactics for training one dog to be motionless whilst the other was being worked around him. One of these was to shed the sheep and put half of them into the corner of the paddock and let the dog stay there whilst I worked the other dog all over the course close by. I would also leave the dog in the middle of the field and drive the sheep around him whilst keeping him down. These techniques were good for keeping the dogs in one place, especially whilst penning the second pen. One of the best brace handlers ever I witnessed was the late David Murray of Peebles, working his two dogs Vic and Number. They weren't free flanking dogs but they were very good followers and they could put up a run that was just about perfection – to me, it was ideal brace work.

## Look or Turn Back

After about six months' work experience I introduced Dick to the 'Look Back'. This is a command that tells him there are sheep behind him that I want him to go back for. It is important not to introduce this too soon so as not to confuse the dog. I have often run Nursery dogs for the first season without having them understand the Look Back command.

Only the last fifteen dogs in the Supreme Championship or World Championship Finals are required to perform this task in a trial environment to test the dog to its limits. However, this skill is though used in everyday work on a mountain or in fields. Sometimes ewes get hidden behind rocks or bushes and while the dog is coming forward on his Fetch, two or three sheep seem to appear out of nowhere behind the dog. So, what you do is give him his Look Back command which can either be a whistle or voice command. But if the sheep can't be seen by the dog, then you need to give the dog either his right or left hand command to re-direct him to the vicinity of the sheep.

I always begin to train the Look Back when Shedding. I cut off a few sheep and let the dog drive them off about twenty yards, stop him, and then when I am close beside him, coax him to turn around and look at the sheep that are left behind. While doing this I tell him to 'look back'. For the first few lessons I do not worry which side he runs out to, as long as he gets behind the sheep and fetches them back to the other sheep. This is a job which does not need to be rushed.

When returning a young dog, always be sure that the sheep are in a position so he can collect them. Nothing frustrates a young dog more than being sent back for sheep that are too difficult for him to collect.

When my dogs have learned their Turn Back whistles properly, I do not stop them when turning them back. This way I get a better redirect and a nicer cast on their Outrun.

After Dick understood the Turn Back command or whistle, I gave him a flank command when returning for his sheep, to give him his first small lesson in redirection. I always make sure before turning a young dog back that I have him flanked into a position where the sheep are directly behind him. By this I mean the handler, the sheep that he is holding, and the sheep that he is going back for are all in a straight line. This makes redirection easier for an inexperienced young dog.

For the first few months after learning the Turn Back, I always make sure that the sheep he is returning for are in sight and teach him to flank on whichever side I ask him on the way back. This is good practice for later in his career when asking him to take his flanks going back on the blind to collect sheep unseen. If I give him his 'Come Bye' command at this stage in his training and he starts to come in, I would stop him on his Outrun. It is very important to be able to stop your dog on his Outrun. I would walk to where he is stopped and stand slightly in front of him, and give him his Come Bye command again to open him out. A few lessons doing this on both the left and right hand commands saves a lot of confusion in a young dog in the initial stages of 'going back on the blind', until he picks up the general idea.

One of the easiest dogs I taught this to was Dick. He quickly figured out that wherever he was turned back from, the sheep were directly behind. Even if sheep are cut off and driven away from me for some distance, when given his return, he would come back towards me and collect the sheep which were left behind.

I think that this part of training a dog should be done over a period of time, with work experience.

## Precision Tuning

To train for precision handling I usually use three sheep, or a ewe with a pair of lambs of at least two months' old, so that every small movement of the dog can be read in the sheep. This is a method I not only used for training Dick but one I have found to work with all types of dogs.

One of the most important skills for a dog to learn in precision training is the 'short flank' – a small sideways movement to correct the sheep's direction of movement at an early stage. This was Dick's final piece of training to polish him off for trialling. Short flanks, in my opinion, are essential to make a top class run. When a dog has reached this standard and the handler is watching the leading sheep, he may only have to flank slightly to keep the sheep in a straight line. This makes for a good flowing run. I do not like to see dogs being stopped on their drives and fetches, preferring to have the pace speeded or slowed according to the sheep.

To get these small flanks I give the dog just a little bit of his whistle command and the more flank I need, I give him more of the full command accordingly. I find that most dogs come on to this short flank training fairly easily.

When a dog reaches this standard it is good practice for the handler to watch the sheep rather than the dog. The big advantage with short flanks is that the slightest movement off line of the leading sheep can be counteracted, and makes for a top class flowing run.

An advantage of short flanks is that the dog does not have to be stopped to deal with sheep getting off line. By working the lead sheep, the flock move together in a more streamlined way.

*Lagnaha Farm and Loch Linnhe from Byn Vair.*

# STORIES & SHENANIGANS FROM FARM AND TRIAL

## A Move to Millisle & the Copeland Islands

In the late 1960s, we broke with tradition and made a move from Shanaghan to a dairy farm on the eastern shores of the 'Ards Peninsula in County Down. A place called Millisle. On a clear day Port Patrick in Scotland is visible across the Irish Channel. The farm is right at the coast, just across the road from the beach – an ideal move as far as my young family were concerned. We joked that, being so close to a village, they were now 'townies' and would need to sharpen up their act. Their ragamuffin days were over.

Millisle was a nice quiet village to live in during the winter, but in summer local caravan parks would fill with people on holiday, mainly from Belfast, and then the village became very busy. As we lived beside one of the busiest caravan parks, there were problems with gates being left open and rubbish being dumped. Broken bottles were a particular problem – which puts me in mind of a friend of mine who had a farm on the slopes of the Mourne Mountains. A camera crew had come to film the scenic town of Newcastle at the foot of the Mournes and to interview some of the local people. When asked what the biggest problem was when farming in the Mournes, Sammy's reply was short. 'Ticks and tourists,' was all he said, which probably didn't go down too well with the tourist authority.

It was at Breezemount Farm in Millisle that the first Nursery Sheepdog Trial in Northern Ireland was organised, and the first working border collie auction. It wasn't an original idea as, at that time in the early 1970s, Nursery Trials were being held in Scotland – that is a trial for dogs under three years' old at the 1st January. It was on our way home on the Stranraer to Larne ferry from a Nursery Trial and dog sale at Moniaive in Scotland that Caldwell Hemphill and I decided it was high time we had something similar back home. So it was that twenty-five dogs ran at the first Nursery Trial at Breezemount, followed by a second trial at Caldwell's and a final at Jimmy Crothers' farm in Banbridge – the final being a competition between the top ten dogs from the first two trials. An auction was held after the trial in Breezemount, the auctioneer being Sam Foster from Banbridge, the top price on the day being 250 guineas for one of Jonathan Irvine's dogs. Nursery Trials are now very popular and well established with National, European and US championships.

About two years after moving to Millisle, I got a lease on the Copeland Island, a 366-acre island about two miles off-shore at Donaghadee, a neighbouring coastal town. The island had quite a large population at one time, but the last residents left in 1942. Back then there had been five family farms, mainly owned by Cleggs, Emersons or Palmers, many of whom are buried in the cemetery on the island. When I took up the lease, nine houses were still kept in a good state of repair – mostly leased by business people from Belfast and Donaghadee and used as holiday homes – one of which was for my use.

The only way to take sheep out to the island was by boat and I made arrangements with a local boat owner to act as a ferry to take stock on and off the island. This involved the dogs working the sheep in the water and driving them onto the shore, an exercise that was filmed the first time I was included in the BBC programme, *One Man and his Dog* back in the 'seventies. That film was used again in the late 'eighties and then early 'nineties, when I was asked to compete on the same programme again. William Lennon was the owner of that boat *The Boy James*, which was able to carry about 120 sheep at once.

When I leased the island there had not been any sheep stock on for a few months, so I had to restock it completely. Unfortunately I could not get the type of stock I really wanted. I would have liked to have had Lanark Newton Stewart type of blackface sheep, as they were going to spend all their time on the Island and grazing would be sparse in the winter. Smaller compact sheep suit these conditions best. The late Ben Wilson, brother of JM who I refer to when talking about sheepdog trialling, told me that a smaller sheep grown to its full potential was a much better sheep than a big sheep stunted. Before the Bluefaced Leicester came to Ireland to breed Mules, the only type available in numbers was the large Perth type of Blackface sheep. This was a type I did not really favour. But, as I had no real choice, I stocked the Island with them, buying some in Donegal, some in Draperstown and some in Antrim.

I made sure though that the first rams used on these ewes were from Ben Wilson of Troloss in Scotland. Mr Wilson was the top Blackface sheep breeder in Scotland in his time and was responsible with his brother JM for taking Newton Stewart sheep to Lanark and developing the Lanark type sheep. I met Ben each time I went to Newton Stewart Ram sales and we kept in touch regularly by phone. He came over with the first ram that I had bought for the Island. I just got a glimpse of the ram coming off the boat from Scotland, as he had to go to the Government Quarantine Station for a month. Ben spent the day with us in Millisle and over the years he told me a lot about JM's way with dogs.

One of the most enjoyable nights I have had was over dinner with Ben and Sir William Young in Lanark. Sir William Young was a master breeder of dairy cattle, Blackface sheep and Border Leicester sheep at Skerrington Mains, Ayrshire. These two men were very able speakers and the evening went very quickly. Sir

William Young was so highly thought of in the agricultural world that there is a bronze bust of him in the Royal Highland Show Grounds.

Another great character in the Blackface sheep world was a close friend of Ben Wilson. He was Jack Kay of Burncastle. There's a story told about him being approached by a shepherd to whom he had sold a dog. Unfortunately the dog had drowned in a flooded river. When telling Jack of the tragedy, he asked if Jack could supply him with a new dog. Jack said yes, but he would cost £500. 'That's twice the price of the last one,' said the shepherd. 'Yes, but this one can swim,' was Jack's reply.

As part of the lease deal on the Island, I had use of one of the houses where I stayed for three weeks at lambing time. This was a very basic three-room stone cottage with an outside toilet and a big open hearth for a fire. Keeping the fire alight at night was never usually a problem as there was a lot of timber washed

up on the shore, especially after a boat had been launched at the shipyard in Belfast. During wartime, one of Kelly's coal boats had sunk off the back of the island and thirty years later, coal was still being washed in from the wreck. So anyone who had time to spare could just pop down to the shore to gather logs and a bucketful of coal for the evening.

Spring time on the island was an interesting time of the year, the first year being the most difficult as the sheep were getting acclimatised to their new conditions. As time went on the sheep that were bred on the island were much more suited to the conditions and I was surprised to see that at low tide, those bred on the island would go out to the rocks and eat seaweed.

The biggest problem at lambing time was the large black back seagulls and grey back crows. If a weak lamb was not seen soon after lambing, it would be the victim of these birds. Part of the island had been cultivated when occupied and there were rigs left by the plough. If a sheep got into one of these on their back, the grey crows would very quickly take out their eyes unless I was able to rescue them in time.

It was hard work at lambing time and the dogs were kept busy. We were not accustomed to having much company on the island through the week, but on one occasion the army came ashore for a look around. As I came over the brow of a hill I was met by a soldier with a Labrador search dog. He didn't take time to ask how the lambing was going, but just shouted at me to get my two sheepdogs under control. I gave Jim and Sweep a little hiss and they both lay down immediately. 'Now you get your dog under control,' I replied. But he wasn't up for a trial and just walked on.

One morning at lambing time I was taking a walk round the island. I was fairly pre-occupied and, not having spoken to anyone for some days by now, was feeling fairly remote from the outside world. When I went round the south end of the island my reverie was interrupted. There, far up on the shore was the bow of a container boat where it had run aground early that morning. It seemed to me to be a fairly brutal intrusion. My isolation was soon over when a salvage team was brought in to remove the containers. There was much debate and consternation before they concluded that they would have to wait until high spring tide to make any move to salvage the cargo and float the ship. In fact it was three weeks before she could be towed into Harland and Wolfe's shipyard in Belfast for repair. When it was prised off the shore there were gaping holes in the side of the boat and only by pumping balloon-type material into the hull to block these holes, was she was made seaworthy for the trip to the shipyard. I was glad to see that boat leave.

# Jim

It was when I had begun to stock and farm the Copeland Islands that I had the help of a dog called Jim. He was a very talented trial dog as he demonstrated by winning the Irish National in both 1974 and 1977 and qualifying for the Irish team at the International Championship five times in succession. But he was also a very gifted working dog and something of a character in his own right. Always very entertaining company.

One of Jim's pet likes was boats. When I let him out of the Land Rover at Donaghadee to go to the island, he would fly down the harbour as fast as he could run and jump onto the first boat he saw. While we were at sea, he would sit on the very point of the boat and, no matter how high the waves were, he was happy to ride them. There were times when you'd have thought he could easily have been washed overboard, but he never was. He just stood looking ahead, often eyeing seagulls about half a mile in front of the boat. He'd stare hard and sway his body as if trying to get them under his control. But once we reached the island he didn't give them a second glance. It just seemed to be something he did to entertain himself while he was on the water.

Back home in Millisle, Wilma had a Cairn Terrier, Paddy, which Jim had great sport with. If Paddy ventured out into the yard, Jim would tease him until Paddy was beside himself, herding Paddy like a sheep round the yard and finally driving him back into the house. Anyone who has ever met or known a Cairn Terrier will know they are very proud dogs with plenty

to say for themselves. It all made for a fairly comical war of personalities. Paddy would really lose his temper, but there was absolutely nothing he could do about it, for Jim was the boss and they both knew it.

Bringing sheep off the island involved loading them onto the boat, *The Boy James*. Very often one or more of them would slip and fall into the water. Whether it was the shock, the cold or just a characteristic of sheep when they hit water, once in the sea they seemed to lose all sense of direction. More often than not they'd swim off out to sea instead of back towards the shore. On occasions when this happened, Jim would leap into the water to swim out around the confused and frightened sheep and herd it back in towards the land, something he loved to do. A sort of aquatic outrun and fetch.

At the back of the island, three small peninsulas went out into the sea. If I put a dog down to bring the sheep off these peninsulas, very often the sheep would jump into the water, thinking they were safer there, before the dog could get around them. But Jim soon figured out that rather than go down the peninsula, he should swim out to the point of the first peninsula. This brought the sheep up the peninsula away from him. He could have then jumped up onto the point and followed the sheep from behind, but no, he was too busy swimming to the second headland to repeat his success with the sheep there. By the time he got to the third peninsula all the sheep had already come back. He figured out this little performance for himself. It was certainly very effective and probably a bit of fun for him too.

He loved the water and, on weekends when the fishing boats brought day-trippers out to play on the island's sandy beaches, Jim would join in any ball games underway in the water. The sport for Jim was to steal the ball away from the children and take it a safe distance away to prove he was the boss. He'd stand there with the ball at his feet and wait for his playmates to come and get it again so the game could carry on. Although a hard working dog, he had a very pleasant nature and was always able to make his way into the company of strangers with great ease. If he saw a family enjoying a picnic, he'd just amble over with his tail wagging and join in the party. In no time at all he'd be rewarded with a nice piece of meat or a tasty sandwich, a treat I was in no position to give him if I was on the island for lambing. He became well known to these visitors who began to look out and ask after him on their occasional trips to the Copeland Island.

When we were gathering sheep to give them their final medicines before lambing time, there were often one or two weak ones that could not keep up with the rest of the flock. When that happened, I would go ahead to the pens with the strong sheep with the help of whatever other dog I had with me, but leave Jim with the weak ones. Jim would work his way back to the pens on his own with these lame or weaker sheep. Sometimes it would take him up to two hours. He let these sheep set the pace, only moving forward to the pens when they moved in the right direction, but blocking any movement by a simple shift of his body if they were in danger of ambling in any other direction. It was a job he loved, coaxing those invalids. And he was a master at it. He just tickled them along. He never put any pressure on them but made sure they made it to the pens in the end for their medicine. Many a time I would sit and admire him coming slowly towards us with his charges and wish that I could have caught it on film.

On the other hand if there was a stubborn, fighting sheep

that wasn't weak, or an old ram that just didn't want to move, he could walk right up to its nose and make it walk backwards for hundreds of yards.

The first trial I won with him was at the Spring Show in Dublin. It was actually the first time I competed with him. I had got him in October and this trial was in the following May. He had got a stubborn old sheep that faced up to him again and again. Jim won though. He backed her the whole way across the cross drive and round to the pen – that's a distance of about 300 yards – with his nose right up against her, and without opening his mouth to nip or grip her. If I had given him the command to 'grip' he would have nipped her on the nose as you often have to do in a working situation, but gripping is not allowed in sheepdog trials so his stare and presence had to do the job on its own. He had power and he knew how to use it. He could 'hit heavy' or he could 'hit light', but he only showed how strong he really was when he had to. Gentle with the weak sheep, intimidating with the stubborn ones.

Being such a good trial and working dog, Jim was in strong demand as a stud dog. It was a job he enjoyed, maybe a bit too much. One Easter week we were on the island for the lambing; a time when the holiday folk were in their houses on the island. When I was walking across the island one morning I met one of these visitors, Liz Wells, who had a pet dog, a cocker spaniel, running around about the house. I stopped to speak to her and unknown to her the bitch was in heat. But Jim had not been so slow and thinking he had a job to do, was more than a bit surprised when we both jumped at the pair of them, getting the spaniel to safety just in time. The next day when I saw Liz again she waved and told me she had the problem solved. Jim ran down to investigate. When I saw what she'd done I was laughing so hard I had trouble calling Jim off. The wee dog was sporting a pair of ladies' knickers tied on with string and was as comical a sight as you can imagine. Mind you, if I hadn't managed to get Jim under control, it wouldn't have been long until he'd have helped her out of them.

Jim enjoyed his life and lived to the ripe of age of sixteen and a half.

## Ronnie Ram

I struck up friendship with a number of the folk who had holiday houses on the island.

One was a chap called Hughie Brown who spent many weekends on the island with his wife Aggie. I used to take a bottle of black rum out with me at lambing time and I would have had a glass every night when I came in to revive me until I got the dinner ready. This particular week Willy Lennon had put me on the island on a Sunday night as he set off to fish for the week. There being no pier as such, I just jumped off the big fishing boat and, on this occasion, managed to break my bottle of rum. All I had left was a bottle of ginger cordial for the week. At night I would have lit the fire and then I got the dinner going and the potatoes boiled – but no black rum.

A few days into my stay, the army came onto the island and broke into all the houses as part of a security search. Once they had searched the houses they left a leaflet of what damage was done and where to apply to get compensation. So it struck me that one of the folk who kept a holiday cottage, Hughie Brown, always had a bottle of brandy in his welly under the stairs. So off I went away down to his cottage. Sure enough, the army had left the door open so I purloined the bottle of brandy to see me through to the end of the week. The army left word with the local police to let the householders know that they had been over. So they all came over the next day and I went down to meet Hughie and his wife. Hughie made a bee-line for the wellington boot – and the brandy was gone.

'God curse them,' he says. 'They've taken my bloody brandy. We'll ha'ta claim for that, Aggie.'

One of the island's biggest characters was an Englishman called Ronnie Ram. He was a Norfolk man and very interesting. He, his wife Dora, their son and his family and a couple called Michael and Heather Reid spent most of their spare time on the island and were great company.

It was Ronnie who told me that the island had a ghost; apparently an old grey-haired woman carrying a basket. There are those who claim to have seen her, but in all my time on the island I never did. Ronnie told me that one evening after dark, when they were on holiday on the island and were sitting at the fire, there was a knock at the door. On opening the door they found a lady with a little girl in some distress. She told Ronnie that her husband was still on board their yacht which had run aground at the south side of the island. She went on to explain that after coming ashore to look for help, she had met an old lady carrying a basket and had approached her to find out where they were. The old lady had told her that she was on the Copeland Island. Ronnie and Dora looked at each other in surprise, knowing no one else was on the island. Given the urgency of the moment they said nothing, but instead accompanied the lady back to the yacht and helped her husband secure the boat for the night.

When Ronnie woke the next morning he looked out and saw the yacht had managed to float on the morning high tide and was by now approaching Donaghadee Harbour some two miles away. He jumped out of bed in a race to get over to Donaghadee to quiz the people on the yacht about their sight of this mystery woman. By the time Ronnie got his boat launched and out to sea, the yacht was already sailing back out of Donaghadee and heading south. He never did find out who they were and so the mystery of the Old Grey Woman was never explained.

Many of Ronnie's relations, including his father, were

gamekeepers on large shooting estates in Norfolk. Ronnie himself was a keen shooting man and owned a most valuable gun which his father had given him. It was a Churchill, still in the original case. There was a history with this gun. Apparently a past editor of the *Shooting Times* had committed suicide with it and his widow had given it afterwards to Ronnie's father on the condition that she would never see it again.

Ronnie's brother-in-law was gamekeeper on a large estate in Norfolk and often invited Ronnie and Dora to the last shoot of the season and to the social evening for the gamekeepers and beaters.

At one particular shoot Royalty attended and Ronnie's brother-in-law asked his wife to take Dora to the best vantage-point to see the vehicles of the Royal Party arriving. They both took their position and waited in anticipation. Dora and her sister-in-law saw more than they planned to, as the first thing on the minds of quite a few of the royal party on getting out of their vehicles was to answer the call of nature – oblivious, of course, to the curious eyes around them.

Ronnie told me that Prince Charles was just a boy then and Ronnie was privileged to look after him during the shoot. He had to peel an apple for him and the only knife he had was one he used to cut his tobacco and skin the occasional rabbit with. He did peel the apple, however, and the Prince was none the worse of it.

I was sharing stories with Ronnie one night over the fire, when he told me the story of a small terrier dog he had grown very attached to during wartime. Ronnie had served on a destroyer in the Royal Navy during the second world war. He came ashore at Aberdeen and he and other crew members were in a bar having a drink, when he noticed a small terrier dog sitting at the bar. Ronnie watched and teased him for a while and seeing he was a bit of a character, he slipped him under his jacket and took him back on board the boat and off back to sea. Ronnie christened the dog Tiny. When the Captain found out the dog was on board, he was very annoyed and demanded he be set free when they next reached land. But it wasn't long before he got very friendly with the dog, as did everyone else on board. When the ship docked, the dog would take the opportunity to go for a run around on shore, but always returned to the ship before it sailed. On one occasion though, he was spied coming running down the pier just after the ship had set sail. Rather than leave Tiny behind, the captain ordered the ship to be turned around to collect him – something he would never have done for a crew-member. After about two years at sea, Tiny took a bad fall with the result that his back was broken and he had to be put to sleep. The Captain ordered that he be buried at sea with full military honours. Just one of the many stories Ronnie told me of his travels during our evenings on the Island.

## Logan's Low Loader

The only transport I had on the island for the first year was a wheelbarrow. I had an old petrol Land Rover at home that was quite good mechanically and a friend of mine, Ray Davidson, had the idea to take it to the island. But getting it there was a problem until Ray came up with the idea of making a raft – a sort of miniature roll-on, roll-off ferry which could be towed behind the boat out to the island. The raft was made of barrels lashed with rope to scaffolding planks. We drove the Land Rover onto the raft very early one morning. Conditions were good and the sea was like a mill pond so the Land Rover was successfully towed onto the Island.

There was some work to be done, so I stayed on the island. After dark I started the Land Rover and drove around with the lights on. I didn't spare a thought as to how strange this sight would be for the folk on the mainland at Donaghadee. Never before had there been lights on the Copeland Islands and it wasn't long before news got around that aliens had landed.

Lots of timber was washed ashore and with a large piece of marine plywood and two planks, I made a sledge to tow behind the Land Rover. People who came over to their holiday homes called this Logan's Low Loader and it served many purposes, such as taking feeding stuff for the landings and bringing wool to the boat. It was also useful for drawing seaweed from the shore to Ronnie Ram's garden to grow potatoes. Every one of the householders on the island had the use of it and some of them even used the Land Rover as a taxi service for people with 'mobility problems' – especially going home from parties. Altogether that old Land Rover and Logan's Low Loader were a tremendous success.

## Wildlife on the Copeland Island

There is a very large variety of bird-life and many different kinds of duck on the Copeland Island. Ducks such as shell, eider, mallard, teal and widgeon are a common sight and I became accustomed to the sound of shearwaters coming in after dark, having flown long distances out to sea to feed. There are also a lot of cormorants on the north end of the island and two large seagull colonies, one on the north end and one on the south end.

Some of the seagulls would be very wicked when nesting. One in particular, on the north end, would dive down to the dog and myself when we were walking round during lambing time. It actually hit me on the head and if the dog was helping to catch a sheep, it was so wicked when diving on him that the dog would stop work.

There is also a large colony of seals along the shores of the island. Seals are inquisitive creatures. If I whistled they would pop their heads out of the water to see what was going on.

On one occasion shortly after my tenancy of the island, Michael and Heather Reid invited me to dinner. I left them around eleven o'clock to go back to my own cottage that had affectionately been named 'The Ponderosa'. As I was picking my way in the dark along the grassy paths and overgrown roads cut by the early inhabitants of the island, my heart missed a beat when something let out a loud deep bellow just behind me. I had never heard anything like it before and I can tell you, it gave me a fright. I didn't hang around to investigate but made a point of finding Heather next day and asking her if she had heard the terrible noise. 'Oh, that's just Hector,' she said. I got to know Hector after that. He was a large bull seal that stayed in the bay beside their house.

More than anything, the Copeland Islands had a large number of rabbits; so many, in fact, that they were a nuisance. The ground was laced with rabbit warrens and they had appetites so voracious they managed to eat more grass than the sheep. They not only ate it, but somehow also managed to churn it up and dirty it. The disease mxyomatosis wiped many out at one time, but still the population increased. Perhaps the disease only served to wipe out the weakest, leaving a new super-breed to multiply with impunity.

Many years later I was invited to judge a trial run by Aileen McConnell and her husband on Vancouver Island off western Canada. Aileen was very keen on her dogs and her sheep. She had cheviot sheep. Very, very good sheep. The trial itself was held on a good course overlooking the sea and the white hills of the Rocky Mountains – which are apparently white the year round. A beautiful set-up. A lot of good handlers came over from the mainland and quite a few came over from the Seattle side on the ferry. One old man who came in from Seattle was about eighty years of age, but had only started trialling a few years previously. Despite being eighty, he ran in the novice trials. He didn't figure in the prizes, but he was getting a lot of fun.

Elizabeth held a party for the competitors one night and I got talking to this old guy and sort of sensed that he had a wee bit of a Northern Irish accent. Says I, 'Where do you come from?'

'You would hardly know it,' he says. 'I come from a wee place in County Down called Groomsport.'

Now Groomsport is only a few miles up the road from Donaghadee. You can see the Copeland Islands from there.

He told me he left there when he was about nineteen or twenty. He said times were very hard before he emigrated to the States. To make ends meet, him and his father and one or two others used to slip over to the Copeland Islands, go round the back not to be seen from Donaghadee and then trap a lot of rabbits and bring them back to the mainland. They sold some and ate some of them themselves. Says I, describing the wee bay at the back of the island by name, 'Is that where you went in?'

'It was indeed,' he says with a look of surprise on his face.

'And,' says I, 'did you go up a wee narrow lane where there were a lot of rabbits at the top?'

'I did,' he says. 'How do you know anything about that?'

'Oh,' says I, 'I had a flock of sheep on the Copeland Islands for eight years and I stayed out every spring and lambed them. I know every inch on it.' It took him back so far I could see the tear in his eye.

'No,' he says at last. 'I don't think I ever will be back.'

## Travels with Hughie

It was while I was farming in Millisle and the Copeland Islands that I got the offer of my first trip overseas with dogs. Unlike later journeys across North America, this trip was not to judge a trial, but instead to put on some sheepdog demonstrations in an agricultural show in Belgium in 1975.

It came about as a result of a deputation from the Belgian Government visiting the Spring Show in Dublin at Ballsbridge. They saw me competing with Jim and winning the Invitation Trials at Dublin Show at the main jumping arena and approached me to do demonstrations over a week at their big show in Belgium.

I agreed to go providing I could get a four-dog team put together. I did not want to take my own dogs, as I would not be able to bring them back because of the quarantine restrictions that applied then. So I bought back two dogs that I had previously sold, a third dog off Franky McCullough and the fourth from the late Lionel Pennyfather. I spent about a week getting them ready for the show and working on individual commands.

We flew out to Brussels with the four dogs. Old Hughie Brown of Newtownards decided he would come with me for a holiday. We had a long wait over at Heathrow to get the connection and Hughie over-indulged in the refreshments and spent maybe too long at the wine place. By the time we got to Brussels he was bursting to go to the loo, but I had to go with the dogs to meet the vet to get their rabies jabs.

It was about two hours before I was back and he was in

agony. There was an old chap there with a wee lorry to take the dogs on to where we were staying in the Ardennes – about a hundred miles away. When I got back Hughie says to me, 'This auld bugger,' he says, 'is stone deaf. I'm trying to get sensed into him that I need to know where the Gents is and I can't get a word of sense out of him.' Says I, 'Hughie, he doesn't understand you. Use sign language.' That worked well and we headed off to the loo about a couple of hundred yards away. We had to put ten francs in an old tin box and there was an old woman standing at the door with a mop. She took one look at Hughie, followed him in to where he stood at the urinals and then began mopping round his feet. Hughie says, 'What's she doin' in here?' Says I, 'I think she fancies you.' 'Tell her to get out the hell out of here,' he says and before I can stop him he's away and marching the wrong way up the corridor. I never saw Hughie move that fast before and it was a long time before I ever did again.

So that was my introduction to overseas trips with the dogs. But it got better. We got the dogs loaded up and then headed off for the Ardennes. There was a car for Hughie and me, with a couple of chaps in it who could speak quite good English. They took us to a farm about a quarter of a mile up the road from our hotel and we got the dogs kennelled with the folk who were supplying the sheep for the trial.

When we went back the next morning to see the dogs, the farmer took us about a mile away up in the forest in the Ardennes to see the sheep that we would be using in the show. The sheep had never seen a dog before. They were as wild as March Hares. I knew it was going to be troublesome to do a decent demonstration with them, but I explained that we would need to gather them all in and pick out six sheep for the demonstration. I needed him to put marks on them and put them on their own in a separate paddock.

He had nothing to mark them with and had to go home for paint, but I insisted that he put them in the paddock before he went home, for I knew it would take him half an hour. I took the opportunity to get the dogs working on them while he was away for, not being a sheepdog man, I knew he would not understand their education and there wasn't much time to explain. By the time he came back they were working quite well. He got the marks put on them and the following day was the start of the show.

I had two demonstrations in the main arena on the first day, one in the morning and one in the afternoon. Each one could not be any longer than ten minutes as they had to be fitted in between events. It was quite a nice little earner as I got one hundred pounds a demonstration. At ten pounds a minute this was fairly decent pay in 1975. Plus I had all expenses and a hospitality card which got me food or drink for free. Hughie Brown got one of them too and he made good use of it, too good at times.

The thing that took a bit of getting used to was that there were no toilets for the gents. You just went where you stood and nobody seemed to mind. When you got a few Scotch whiskies it seemed to take the shyness off you.

All in all, we were getting on not so bad. The biggest problem after two or three days demonstrating was that the sheep got so well trained I had to keep the pen gate closed. I always penned them at the end of the demonstration and then transferred them from the pen across the arena to a wee trailer behind the farmer's truck that supplied the sheep. After a while, we had to keep the trailer door closed too for, after being with the dogs for two or three days, if they saw an open door into the trailer they would have been into it in spite of us.

Travelling backwards and forwards between the farm and the show gave us a chance to have a look at the Ardennes countryside. Something that struck me about farming in the Ardennes was the number of farmers living in wee hamlets or villages which we passed. Each morning at about half past six they would all head off on their tractors and trailers away up into the forest. Up there the stock were grazing through the trees – a few acres here and there that wasn't planted. The cows were dairy-type Belgian Blues – to my eye like a half Friesian, half short horn. On their trailers they had a row of creamery cans and the milking machine with the pipeline out round it. They would just pull this equipment into the field and the cows would gather around it. The farmer would then chain them to the trailer, milk them in the fields and then draw the milk home later. It was certainly a different way of life.

The show was a big success and had attracted huge crowds. On the biggest day of the show they reckoned there were 65,000 spectators there. You may guess what it was like with no gents' toilet and only one ladies'.

At the end of the week the government bought the dogs off me and allocated them to their new owners. One of my dogs was a good looking red-coloured dog called Nap, which the Minister of Agriculture gave to a nice blond lady, very well dressed. The interpreter that I had with me said it was rumoured that she was his mistress, so Nap would be well looked after. It was just as well, for the poor old boy was ready to retire.

## Early days at Lagnaha Farm, Argyllshire

In 1979 we sold the farm at Millisle and moved to Argyllshire. Lagnaha is a 3,500 acre hill farm near Ballachulish on the shores of Lough Linnhe and Loch Leven in Argyllshire, one of the most scenic parts of the Western Highlands of Scotland. There are three high peaks on Lagnaha, referred to by the locals as Lettermore, Byn Vair (the 'hill of the thunderbolt') and Glenduror. These peaks are classed as Monroes all being over 3,000 feet.

I actually moved to Lagnaha in January, but Wilma and Jeff, my wife and son, did not come until April, after all the details were finalised in Millisle. The Copeland Islands had a further year until the lease ran out and so the sheep stock remained on the island for that year, which meant there was to be much travelling back and forward. It was a one hundred and eighty mile journey between Lagnaha and the ferry at Stranraer – a winding, very scenic route through Glencoe and along the shores of Loch Lomond.

The night I moved, Sammy Nelson, a friend from Donaghadee who had retired, came with me. Sammy had served as a volunteer lifeboat man for many years and was on a lifeboat which rescued thirty-one passengers off the car and passenger ferry, *Princess Victoria*, which sank in 1953 in the North Channel on a routine crossing from Larne to Stranraer. Of the 176 people on board that night, 133 lost their lives.

Sammy had been a fisherman all his life, but he was coming with me as chief cook and bottle washer. I collected him in Donaghadee with the Land Rover, and a horse-box packed with as many essentials as it would hold, to keep me going until Wilma came over.

The dogs were in the back of the Land Rover and we were just about to leave when a neighbour arrived with a puppy which was a payment for a service for one of his bitches. This too was stowed in the Land Rover and we sailed on the eleven o'clock ferry that night, arriving in Cairnryan at around one in the morning.

There was a lot of fog on our way up and with the Land Rover and trailer loaded, we had not much speed. We arrived at Lagnaha at seven that morning and collected the key from a neighbour John Cameron and his wife Rena. Collecting the key was a formality as it turned out. The door of the house was not locked.

I gave the puppy which I had brought over to Johnny and Rena – they called him Paddy. Paddy lived to be very old. Everyone in the village knew him.

Shortly before moving to Lagnaha, Wilma and I had received an invitation to the leaving party for the Arthurs, the previous

119

owners, which was also a welcoming party for us. John Arthur was a well-respected man in the village. He was on the local show committee and the local sheepdog trials committee, so at the party I was invited to take his place on these committees. There were two communities – those who had retired to the area and the local people who had lived there all their lives. Everyone fitted well together and we were made very welcome.

It transpired that the farm of Lagnaha had quite a pedigree. Robert Louis Stevenson's book, *Kidnapped*, was based in that area. More unsettling is the story of James Stewart who was hanged for shooting the Red Fox, the government tax collector. Once when out gathering sheep I came on a cairn on Lettermore with a plaque claiming that this was the spot where the Red Fox was shot. Around the cairn were the remains of an old road, probably at one time an old drove road. The locals maintained that the person who had actually killed the Red Fox fled to France, but a Stewart had to take the blame and pay the price. Stewart was arrested and taken to Inverary where he was tried and hung for the murder, although it has been told for generations that he was actually ploughing when the murder was committed. His body was brought back to Ballachulish and a monument marks the spot where he was left hanging to disintegrate, until someone buried him in an old cemetery called Keil, about one mile south of Lagnaha. You can still find his grave there. A cave on the hillside behind Lagnaha Farmhouse is reported to have been his place of refuge before his arrest.

At one time there was a granite quarry on Lagnaha and opposite, on Loch Linnhe, there was a small harbour from where apparently a lot of granite stones were shipped at one time. One famous destination was Dublin and I was told by Sandy Campbell, who had a lot of knowledge of that area, that granite shipped from Lagnaha helped to build the Post Office in Dublin, famous as the scene of the Easter Rising.

A few miles north of Duror is the village of Glencoe where the Campbells massacred the McDonalds in their beds early one morning. When I lived in the area there was a sign in the hotel in Glencoe which said, 'No Campbells welcome.'

In contrast to the history of the place and the tranquillity of the hills, low flying military jets were a feature which took some getting used to at Lagnaha. They seemed to appear from nowhere, flying up one glen and down another. When up herding sheep I would often have been looking down on the planes. The noise was unreal and could actually be frightening. Once coming through Glencoe with the Land Rover and trailer, I thought the wheels had come off the trailer until I caught a glimpse of the jet. I imagine it was a great place to perfect your flying skills but it was just somehow out of context.

## Getting to Know the Locals

Lagnaha was situated on the main road between Oban and Fortwilliam, not far from Glencoe and Ballachulish Bridge. There were two village shops, one at Duror, which was the local post office and one at Kentallen. Lagnaha Farm surrounded Kentallen village, so I would be at the shop most mornings after feeding the sheep. I got to know the shopkeeper well and she liked plenty of news, so I made sure I gave her plenty, never putting her off with a bad answer. She always asked me when my wife would be coming over to the point that I got tired of this question. When she asked again I told her that if she didn't come soon I would have to look for a new one. 'Oh!' she said. 'It happened in Lagnaha before!' I mentioned this later to Johnny Cameron who told me that a previous owner had made off with the local schoolteacher.

After Sammy cooked us a fry for breakfast and presented a bit of lunch, I was glad to have a change in the evening and would go to the Duror Hotel for dinner. This was a family run hotel a short distance from the farm. Evan Cameron and his wife Kathy owned the hotel and after a short period Kathy and

I became good friends on account of her stock of toilet rolls. As I was coming out of the hotel one evening I stopped to chat to Sandy Campbell, a much respected gentleman in the village, and as we were talking we were being showered with toilet rolls flying out of an upstairs window. I had noticed a hippie-style chap with long hair as I was coming out of the hotel and saw that he was now standing in the road as if waiting for someone. I went into the hotel and informed Kathy that there were a lot of toilet rolls outside, wondering if there were children playing in the toilets. 'Oh,' she said. 'Bad luck to them. It's them hippies.' She then went into the storeroom and caught a girl in the act. The chap that Sandy and I had seen in the road could not gather them up as we had been chatting at the door. After that, when Sammy and I went for a meal, we got the very best attention.

On one occasion I had notice to attend a sheepdog trial meeting due to be held in Appin School at eight o'clock one evening. Appin is eight miles south of Duror towards Oban. I set off early, but for a long time no one arrived. I later learned that Appin is like the west coast of Ireland where if you say eight o'clock, then you are understood to mean nine. To kill time, I took a tour around the area and popped into the Creagan Inn where there was an elderly lady behind the bar and two gentlemen drinking. One of these men I got to know very well, Ronnie McCall. When I went into the bar and ordered a drink, the two men saw that I was a stranger and the conversation stopped while they measured me up. When they heard me speak they realised I was Irish so one of the men, who turned out to be Ronnie McCall, said, 'What's your business in this part of the world?'

'Ah,' I said, 'I'm looking for second-hand guns. Where I come from they're very scarce, there is so much demand for them.'

'You wouldn't be the new man in Lagnaha would you?'

'You wouldn't be far away,' says I.

With that, he gave the lady behind the bar a nod and up

comes another drink and we got into conversation. I never did get to the sheepdog meeting that night.

I got to know Ronnie though and that he had a contracting business and a small farm or croft as they are known in the Highlands. He had quite a few employees. He told me that there was a burn on Lagnaha and that he had an agreement with the previous owner, John Arthur, to take two loads of gravel from there each month when doing drainage work. He asked me if I would be agreeable to continue to sell him the gravel. I said that when two Scotsmen had made a deal, it would do me fine. Money was never mentioned but every month Ronnie would reach down into the bib pocket of his dungarees and pay in cash what was owed. I would say, 'Ronnie, leave it for a few months and it will be worthwhile.' But he insisted on his monthly payments.

## Bill Black the Travelling Salesman

A few weeks after I came to Duror, Jeffrey, our second son, followed to help farm Lagnaha. My other children had by now all flown the nest, my eldest son Alan a teacher, Jeff's twin sister Jennifer a nurse and the youngest, Joanne, at Queen's University back in Belfast.

On our first spring I had to return to the Copeland Island for lambing, leaving Jeff and my chief cook, Sammy, on their own.

While I was away, a travelling salesman called by. His name was Bill Black and when in the area he stayed in the Duror Hotel. It did not take him long at the bar to find out from the locals that the ownership at Lagnaha had changed. So he popped by to let Jeff know that he had supplied the previous owner with veterinary products, dog food and the like and to ask if he could expect to continue to supply us. Not wanting to commit us in my absence, Jeff explained that I was still farming sheep back in Ireland. Hearing we were farmers from Ireland,

Bill warmed to the subject and says to Jeff, 'You wouldn't know Harford Logan at all, would you?'

'Aye,' says Jeff. 'Sure that's my dad.'

Now Bill and I had met a long time back in the 1960s at an International Sheepdog Trial in Stirling. James Brady and I were on the Irish team and, true to form, had not been organised enough to get any accommodation booked, relying on our past success of just sorting something out at the time. I spoke to the chap who was taking the sheep to the exhaust pen and asked if he would know of any bed and breakfast accommodation. 'Yes,' he replied. 'My wife does bed and breakfast. It's quite a journey but I go home every night.' That was our introduction to Bill and we decided to go home with him.

On the way back to Bill's place at Drymen, we stopped at a small inn in Bulquivie village for refreshments and while discussing the day's trialling, Bill suddenly remembered he was due to play a cheili that night. That was how we found out that Bill had a dance band, in fact it was quite famous. His wife and two sons all played and the band was known all over Scotland.

During our time at Lagnaha Bill stayed with us when in the area. We had some good conversation which would go well into the night. One night the telephone rang quite late and it was Wilma who had been having some friends in at Millisle and had rung to see how we were doing. I said I had a dance band in the house. She had more expected me to be curled up in my bed. Bill always carried his accordion and fiddle; he was a good musician on any instrument. I asked her what type of music she would like Bill to play and she requested a tune on the accordion. So Bill played the tune. 'What is going on,' she said, 'or who have you in? You'll have the place wrecked!' I said, 'If you can have a party, we can have a party as well.'

Bill and I have remained close ever since. In fact, when the band was playing in Duror Hall across the road from Lagnaha, they would have always stayed with us.

# Wildlife at Lagnaha

Occasionally we would have seen red deer on Lagnaha, but more often there were roe deer down low and around the house and garden. These could be a nuisance, as they would eat shrubs and be generally destructive. Whilst they are native to England, Scotland and Wales, roe deer are not found in Ireland. In fact neither are moles or snakes.

Although red deer were quite rare on Lagnaha, many neighbouring farms and estates had large numbers of them. A neighbour who lived a short distance away, sowed a small field of oats and when they had grown to around four inches, the field was invaded by red deer who cleared the lot. As the nearest herd of deer was based about five miles away, they must have had scouts looking out, or else had smelt the growth from a long distance.

If you were driving after dark, a red deer could run across the car lights and cause a nasty accident, especially through Glencoe and over Rannoch Moor. Even the small roe deer could be dangerous running across the road at night. The eyes of the deer shine brightly in the car lights, so if the eyes of one deer are seen, there would be many following.

There are many buzzards in the area which tourists would have mistaken for eagles. There was, though, a pair of eagles on Lagnaha that stayed out on Glen Duror. They were not to be seen flying low but were always high in the sky. Although there are problems in some areas with lambs being lost to eagles, we never had any with the residents of Lagnaha.

Occasionally I would even see wild Highland cats. I am told that these native cats are impossible to tame. Not that I wasted too much time trying.

# Farming Lagnaha

The sheep stock on Lagnaha were Lanark/Newtown Stewart; a type popular on the high hills up the West Coast.

I rented a further two hundred acres on nearby Keil Estate, grazed cattle there during the summer months and lambs in winter.

We did not disturb the sheep on the hills much at lambing time, but we kept a close eye on the fox dens for any activity. If there was any sign of dead lambs we would get in touch with Jimmy Jackson, who was employed by the Fox Club during lambing to deal with foxes with his terriers.

Over the years on these high hills, nature has bred out the strains of sheep with lambing difficulties, which has resulted in little loss during lambing. I'm told that nature is given a helping hand in New Zealand where, if any of the flock have had a difficult lambing, they are culled. They consider it a matter of working with nature rather than against it.

One heft of sheep on Lagnaha was given feed blocks during the winter on Byn Vair, as the grazing was not as good there as on the rest of the hills. These feed blocks were purchased from a company that also supplied a helicopter to distribute them in half-ton bags across the hill. This was the only way to get feed out to sheep on these high hills. I would go up with the pilot and show him where to drop off the bags. The whole locality would be done in one day. The ground crew would hitch the bags on to the helicopter and when one farm was finished they went on to the next. From the first of February onwards we would go around the bags and put out enough blocks to feed the sheep for a week.

The rams were not put to the ewes until the 28th November. This was a time when the dogs got a lot of work. A lot of colour was put on the rams so they were easily spotted on the hill. If we spotted two together, we would split them and take one back to where it should be. This was good experience for young dogs that were well forward in training.

New young rams, or tups, were always brought in after being out for three weeks. These young sheep would have been well fed to have them in top form for the sales, so it was advisable to bring them in before they lost too much weight.

Star got badly hurt when bringing in a tup once. It was at the end of January and I was out on Glenduror when, with the binoculars, I saw a tup high up on the ridge. Star would run out long distances on the hill and on that particular occasion he had about three hundred yards of forest to go through before he reached the open hill. He then had to negotiate a waterfall which, on that day was frozen. He slipped on the ice and fell about forty feet down the hill smashing his pelvis. He didn't work for a long time and when he did recover, I found that his nervous system had been affected. He was never the same dog, even at trials. He had already won the Scottish National some months previously but as a result of this accident and despite his being a young dog, I retired him early from trialling.

I had a very good team of three dogs at Lagnaha; all three were National winners, Jim having won the Irish National twice, Sweep once and then Star who won the Scottish National in the following year. I regret not having a photograph of the three of them together.

The first sheep gathering of the year was always the most difficult. This was to mark the lambs in June. We would know then how many lambs we had and the lambing percentage for that year. It was interesting to see the quality of lambs from different rams. It took approximately three days for three of us to gather Lagnaha. If the weather was warm the dogs would quickly get tired, so one dog was kept rested during the gathering. When coming in with the flock of sheep at the end of the gather there was the odd ewe who would try to escape

into the bracken with her lamb. So a fit dog was needed to
keep them under control.

The next gathering was in July for the shearing, which was
done by contractors. But the weather could be a problem in
July, with often rain and mist on the hill making it impossible
to get the sheep that were high out.

After shearing they were dipped and dosed and put back
to the hill until sale time in September. Stock ewe lambs were
selected and the rest of the lambs and cast ewes were taken to
sheep sales in Dalmally and Stirling.

There were always a few sheep missed at the July sheep-
shearing gathering. These would usually come in with the
September gather and would have to be sheared ourselves by
hand. Ruaridh MacDairmud, or Roddy as he was known, was
a good help for me. He was a contract shepherd, so as well as
gathering and all the work involved with the sheep, he did a
lot of fencing on Lagnaha.

In October we winter-dipped the stock ewes and stock lambs
which were going off for wintering. It was at this stage that we
marked the sheep. If you see a flock of sheep, you will notice
that they each have the same colour mark in more or less the
same place; maybe on the shoulder, the back or the rump. This

is made with a substance called keel, hence what we call a 'keel mark', and the mark is there to help identify one farmer's sheep from another. The mark lasts about a year before the weather washes it out but, unlike paint, it does not damage the wool. I tended to use a red mark, my neighbours used blue. When I was out on the hill after dipping time and noticed any sheep without a keel mark, I would bring them in to be dipped and marked. This way we were able to keep a count of the flock. There were always some strays in the gathering belonging to neighbouring hills, which I would hold in a paddock until they came to collect them. Often they would have strays belonging to Lagnaha and would bring them back to me – a simple system that worked well, our neighbours being good honest people.

## Some Trials on the Scottish Islands

Although I had been competing and judging trials for nearly thirty years by the time I arrived in Lagnaha, I always consider my real apprenticeship began during these years I spent in Scotland, competing in and judging trials all over the Highlands and Islands. The real experts were the old-time handlers and judges I met there, many of whom were retired shepherds and a few who were old but far from retired. These were very practical men and their decisions made much sense. They could always give a reason for what they had done.

I judged on the Isle of Lewis, which is about two hours by boat from Ullapool. I found Lewis a bleak island with few trees, but the people are very hospitable and friendly. I stayed with a gentleman called Mr MacLeod who had a hand-weaving loom in the garage. Many of the islanders had hand looms and made tweed which they sold to manufacturers. Weaving is a time-consuming job, but was a way of life on Lewis.

I also judged a trial in Shetland, motoring to Aberdeen and spending fourteen hours on the ferry to Lerwick. I had four dogs with me as the judge was required to do a demonstration. I stayed with a gentleman called Cecil Nicholson who had a dairy farm on the island. Cecil took me on a tour of the island, parts of which were still being farmed in the old-fashioned way. I saw one farmer cutting hay with the scythe and some shearing sheep with hand shears. He showed me Shetland Beds that were used before central heating was common. These beds had wooden sides with a roof on top. On one side there was a sliding door which was opened to get in and out of the bed. It looked to me like a coffin on legs. I felt claustrophobic just looking at it.

Cecil supplied milk from his dairy farm to Lerwick. He also had a sizeable sheep flock which consisted of native Shetland sheep, which have naturally short tails and do not have to be docked. He also bred Shetland ponies. It was an interesting farm for me, with a good variety of stock.

I later visited and trialled on the Isle of Islay. One of the handlers on Islay was coincidently called John Logan, although he was no relation. There was no problem going there, but getting home could be difficult, as the people were so hospitable they would want me to stay overnight. Islay is a lovely island with very good farm and hill land. The beaches are beautiful too. Geese come into Islay in their thousands in the autumn.

One night when I was having a meal in the Hotel at Bridgend, I happened to admire the murals on the walls. They'd caught my eye being quite large and colourful and depicting scenes from the island. That got me chatting to the manager who suggested that, after my meal, he should introduce me to the man who had painted them. He said he was actually an Irishman like me. So after the meal I was taken away from the tourist side of the hotel and into the public bar where a few local people were having a drink and a chat. There I was introduced to a wee old man sitting at the bar wearing wellies. He was Sean O'Leary and had come to Islay with a boatload of salt. He liked the island so much that he decided to stay and he lived in a caravan nearby and painted.

I talked to other local men in the bar who were fishermen and it was there that I met the chap who bought *The Boy James*, the boat which was featured in the television programme *One Man and his Dog* and which I used to take the sheep to and from the Copeland Island.

I competed a few times on the Isle of Bute. In fact I won trials there twice with a dog called Jean, the mother of one of my very best dogs, Dick. Once the late Ralph Pulfer from Ohio came over to the Isle of Bute with me to compete. Ralph Pulfer was one of the top handlers, or the top handler at that time in the States. He was still winning his share well into his eighties.

Ralph had been visiting the North of England with Raymond MacPherson before he came to me, and Raymond had lent him a dog. He was made very welcome on the island, as all visitors are, and was invited into the hospitality tent and asked what he wanted to drink. He said he would have whatever the rest were having. So he got brandy, a drink he had never tasted before but seemed to like. The hospitality was good and, before he knew it, he'd had quite a few before he went out to compete. The sheep were very flighty, being Blackface Gimmers, and a bit touchy, more than he would be used to in the United States. He got on fairly well round the course, until it came to the shedding ring. Each time Ralph made to take a dive to shed them, the sheep had moved somewhere else. He didn't manage to finish the shed but he really enjoyed himself. On the way home by boat, (the pickup was at the ferry terminal), Ralph was in good form and says to me, 'Harford, what exactly is brandy?' I told him it is reputed to be the 'drink of Kings', so he was determined to take a bottle home to the States.

# Indiana & Burbank

It was not long before I saw Ralph Pulfer again, as it was just at this time that I received my first invitation to judge sheepdog trials in North America. I flew into Toronto and was picked up there by Ivan Weir, originally from Dromore in County Down but who had moved to Canada about thirty years previously.

We motored a long way down to Quincy, Ohio where we stayed with Ralph. The first night we stayed there, he held a great party for us in the cellar of his house. A lot of the competitors came in to join us and were all being very kind to me – possibly measuring me up for the first trial to be held in a big fairground in Indiana in two days' time.

I was sort of nervous on the morning of that trial, thinking about what the sheep would be like and how the competitors would take to my standard of judging compared to what they were used to with American judges. As it happened, I set off for the trial on the truck that was picking up the sheep. That did not help my nerves anything either, for when we arrived to collect the sheep we found they had young lambs with them which they proceeded to lift off their mothers and close in a separate pen.

I was glad I had seen this, for now I knew the mothers would be almost impossible to work with in a trial environment, for they would be fighting the dogs. So on the way back to the trial I kept thinking how these sheep would work. I reckoned there would be a lot of 'gripping' as the dogs would need to face up to these aggressive sheep. Gripping refers to a dog moving into the sheep and using his mouth to grab one, usually the wool or fleece but on occasion the leg or nose. In everyday work you may ask a dog to grip on command, especially if a ewe is being very aggressive, but in the United Kingdom and Ireland a dog will be automatically disqualified in a sheepdog trial if it grips the sheep. So, given the temperament of these ewes, I decided not to disqualify for gripping unless the sheep were being abused.

This turned out to be a sound decision, as by the end of the day I had only one dog that did not grip. That was a dog that I had seen before, having been exported by John Joe Thompson from Broughshane in County Antrim to Ralph's brother, Louis Pulfer. The dog had been winning quite a lot of trials in America and, as it was the only dog that did not grip, I had no problem getting a winner.

Choosing between the rest of them was a bit of a harder job though. All had their fair share of trouble in trying to control the sheep, but I managed to get the judging done without anybody complaining. It had not been the prettiest trial in terms of runs, but it was the first I had judged in America and everybody seemed happy enough.

The next trial on that, my first US trip, was in Burbank. This was one of the biggest sheepdog trials at that time in America; a very high prestige trial which was held over two days. In stark contrast, the sheep at Burbank were very good and the running was really top class – as good as you would have seen anywhere in Ireland or Great Britain. The competitors came from long distances with handlers from Arizona, California, Texas, the Mid West and all over Canada. It was *the* trial at that time in the States – everyone wanted to win Burbank and there was pretty big money for it too. The winner that day was Bob Childress from Texas – a chap I got to know quite well and stayed with at his ranch years later. The prize money must have been quite good, for Bob took all the competitors out for dinner after the trial. Whether that was paid for out of the winning or his oil wells, we enjoyed it anyway.

Between the two trials I had time on my hands, so I agreed to join Ralph and Ivan Weir on a long trip to a country fair in Richmond, Virginia. We started off just before midnight from Ralph Pulfer's place, lifted Jim Bob McKeown at Indiana and an old chap whose company I really enjoyed, Barney Platfoot.

Once on board, the five of us headed off together in a large pick up, double cab, with twin wheels on the back of it – a huge thing. We motored all night non-stop and did not get into Richmond Virginia until five o'clock the following evening.

We stopped for about three breakfasts during that trip, after which we would all settle back into the pickup. I was in the front seat of the cab with two of the others, both of them chewing tobaccy. Each time we stopped to check the dogs or had a break, they were rummaging in the bins for old coke tins to use for spittoons which they would then set up on the dash in front of us. It was just as well the roads were fairly straight, for every time there was a bend I was watching these danged auld tins in case they would tumble over with all these spittles in them. Happily they stayed where they were, but it was a long, long journey and when we eventually arrived at the show in Richmond, Virginia the following evening, I was surprised to discover there was a sheepdog trial in the fairground.

It was only then that they broke the news to me that they had me entered to run in that trial. It was a set-up! They had arranged for me to run a dog that I had exported out to Ivan Weir three years earlier. I didn't know whether the dog would still work for me or not, so 'No,' I told them, I wouldn't run. But they were equally insistent that I would compete.

With no choice but to go ahead, I took the dog on a lead through the fairground and had a look at some things through the show and other events that were going on. The dog just did not seem to know me at all. He was peeing up against this and that until I could put up with it no longer and just about twenty minutes before I was due to go on to compete, I gave him a pluck on the lead and said in a stern voice, 'What do you think you're doing?' He sort of wagged his tail at that familiar command and says I, 'My boy, you're maybe beginning to know me now.'

I kept my fingers crossed as I was called on and introduced as Harford Logan from Ohio. Apparently if they had entered me with my real Scottish address on Public Broadcast, some of the other competitors may have refused to compete, thinking maybe I was a professional. Actually, there were some of them as good as I was, maybe better.

But anyway I went out with the dog, Roy, a dog that I had originally bought as a young six-month old pup from Wales. I got on quite well with him at home, but I just never fell in love with him so I thought somebody else had better have him. I went out to run, and the old bugger, I never saw him running better – he ran foot perfect the whole course and ended up winning the trophy, to the cheers of the boys in the grandstand who had entered me. I have the trophy in the house yet – it was a sort of a gold cup but it was plastic and I told them to treat themselves with the prize money.

We went for a meal in a country club where there was a bit of a dance. We had a good night and the five of us ended up staying in a motel – two got beds, I was lucky enough to be one of them, the other three slept in sleeping bags. We had television and a bathroom and shower and all five of us stayed for the price of a couple – not that I had to pay for anything. I was on a free run. My prize money must have covered all.

It was a very enjoyable run home through the Blue Ridge Mountains. We had missed them on the way to the fair as it was dark. But it was clear on the way home and, as everyone knew their road, no one saw the need to buy a map. We must have got lost about five times, for about five times we saw 'Welcome to West Virginia'. We ended up in Kentucky. It took us one day going, but two days coming home. But it suited me fine, for I was seeing the different lifestyles out through the blue hills – the Shenandoah Valley and the tobacco hanging up in Kentucky. There seemed to be a lot of small farmers and each one of them had a wee tobacco shed with tobacco plants hanging up with the leaves drying. It was nice to see.

# Trouble in Illinois

I was invited out again by Ralph Pulfer to judge trials in the mid-west in Illinois. Ralph picked me up from the airport and we went through to Illinois the day before the trial.

When we arrived apparently things were not going all that smoothly. A guy who had always done most of the organisation, and liked his own way, had been outvoted by the committee who thought they would do it their way this time. They appointed me as judge and thought they had an arrangement for the supply of the sheep. But it did not please the previous organiser and he wanted to supply someone else as judge. He had his own favourites. The night before the trial, the word came through from him that if the trial was to go on, they would have to use his sheep – for the sheep the committee thought they had arranged for the trial had been bought off the dealer by this chap that night. So if they wanted sheep they would have to use his sheep and if they wanted to run a trial they would have to use his judge.

So here was I sitting at nine o'clock at night in the middle of this feud wondering what the heck sort of a place I had landed or how I was going to get out of it with all of the expense of going out there and going home without judging. But anyway there was a chap Eastroy Macausland whose home place was about three or four hundred miles away. He said he thought he could get them out of the difficulty. So he rang home and one of his men got on the road with his sheep. The trailer only held about fifty sheep and to run the trial properly you would have needed about a hundred. But he said they were Barbados and they could be run as often as you liked. I had seen Barbados, but I had never experienced them running in a trial.

We were to start at eight o'clock the following morning, but we had to wait for the sheep that had been motoring all night and which did not arrive until nine o'clock.

These sheep had been well used to dogs, Eastroy being a

keen trialist. And they were very good to handle. Apparently a Barbados can run like a gazelle if it is not well used to dogs. They are a hairy rather than a woolly sheep and you do not have to shear them. They are brown with long legs, more like deer or goats than they are sheep. But they do not seem to tire and they can stand the hot weather. They were run over and over again and, although there were only fifty of them and sixty dogs to run over the two days, they were still as good the last time they ran as they had been the first time.

It was something of an unusual start to a trial but we managed to get over the difficulties. I never heard tell of that old guy since – I expect he's dead now.

## Winning the Scottish National

Back home in Lagnaha at that time in the early 1980s, I had switched allegiance and was now in the Scottish National team. In 1981 I won the Scottish National held at Glamis Castle, the family home of the Queen Mother. In that particular year there had been an unusually big entry of participants, around 180 dogs and the event was held over four days. It all proved too much for the judges and the audience, so, after that, the number of entries in the National Competitions was curtailed to 150 dogs and the event limited to three days.

The Scottish National started on Wednesday and I ran early on Thursday morning, so I had a long wait until Saturday evening to see if I would still hold on to top place. It was a close run thing as strictly speaking the trial got easier and could have been won on the last four or five runs. The problem was that, with all those entries, the organisers ran out of the hill sheep being used and had to bring in much quieter lowland sheep for the last few runs. Not realising the difference, the remaining handlers continued to handle them softly as they would the more unpredictable hill sheep, with the result that they were so kind to them they ran out of time. For a National run, the sheep need to be trotting along at a nice working pace to leave time for finishing. No one in those last few runs made the Final Team.

I won the trial with Star and was also in the Scottish team with Sweep, the dog that had won the Irish National the previous year at the Curragh Racecourse in Co. Kildare.

In the brace class, I had a very good run with old Jim and Sweep. I had a very good course and managed the first pen with Jim without any breaks, then went on to pen the second set of sheep with Sweep. With the weather being fairly warm, Jim, being ten years old and a bit past his best, was feeling the heat of the sun. I left him lying at the mouth of the pen and was just about to pen the second flock when Jim thought, 'To pot with this,' and went and lay down in the shade at the side of the pen, something he had never done in any previous competitions. The result was that the sheep got out of the first pen. If it hadn't been for that, I could have won both the doubles and the singles that day. But I was very delighted to win the Scottish National and so soon after having won the Irish title.

It was the first time the Scottish National cup had been taken home to Lochaber, but it was the start of a run because two years after that Alasdair MacRae, also from Lochaber, won the cup. That was back in the 1980's and no one has taken it there since.

## Scottish Sheep Sales

Sheep sales in Scotland were a new experience for me. In Ireland, if one hundred sheep were for sale, they would be drawn into pens of ten, whereas in Scotland, they would sell all one hundred together in one lot. I found it quite enjoyable following a hundred ewes into the ring rather than ten. The same was true of wether lambs. I have followed two hundred into the ring and sold them as one lot. The most sold together in Ireland would be twenty.

I should explain what I mean by a wether lamb. It's actually a castrated male lamb, or as Master Curry more tactfully explained to a lad in my class, 'God made them rams, your daddy made them wethers.'

Sir William Young told me the story of Ben Wilson showing a tup (ram lamb) when he was a boy at a local show and failing to be in the prize list. On his way home he met a neighbour, but Ben's thoughts were on the show and the lamb. The neighbour greets him, 'Grand weather, Ben.'

'He will be tonight,' replies Ben, clearly resolved as to what to do about that lamb.

Most flock owners take pride in how they present their stock. Cast ewes could have their faces washed and heads oiled before going into the ring and much time is spent selecting lambs to have each batch the same size.

Ram sales in Fortwilliam were a big occasion. It was the local farmers' annual celebration, and they knew how to let their hair down. Friends would meet who had not seen each other since the previous year.

I heard a story of two gentlemen who met up at Fortwilliam sale, both having purchased expensive tups the year before. One enquired of the other, 'How did your tup do?'

'Oh,' he replied, 'bad luck, he died. But how did yours do?'

'Oh,' replied the other, 'I had bad luck too. He lived.'

No matter how careful you are about the ancestry, you can still occasionally buy a bad-breeding tup which can set the standard of a flock back years. In its first year, it is advisable to use a new tup sparingly and if the lambs do not please, then don't use him again, no matter how high the purchase price.

On one occasion when selling rams at Fortwilliam sales, a customer who usually bought one of my best rams every year selected a black-faced ram with a grey nose, which was the best ram in the pen. The only other one with a black face and grey nose happened to be the worst one I had. The customer having made his choice went off to the bar with some friends to wait for my sheep to go into the ring. When my sheep were ready for sale, I sent to the bar for my customer. My number one ram went into the ring and sold for five hundred pounds which I was pleased with having paid forty pounds for him as a lamb the year before. The last sheep into the ring was the other black-faced ram – and my worst one. The way sheep had been selling that day I did not expect to get much of a price, but to my surprise the bids started to go up and reached one hundred and twenty pounds before being knocked down. On hearing the purchaser's name called out, I knew that the customer had over-indulged at the bar and bought the wrong sheep. Speaking to him later in the day when giving him a 'luck penny', he told me he had indeed made a mistake. He was quite sober by then.

## The Irish Scot in Texas

By now I was getting tempting invitations every year to judge trials in North America. It was a temptation I had no intention of resisting and as a result I had the pleasure of experiencing farming and trialling across many states – Texas, Dakota, Montana, Wyoming, California, Pennsylvania, Maryland, Oklahoma and Vancouver to name a few.

I had three trips in all to Texas. The first trip was to judge a trial which was being held during a world championship Rodeo in Waco. I later returned to judge a series of trials called the Winter Olympics and then the Texas Finals in Ozona.

On my first visit to Texas I was picked up from Dallas Airport by a friend of mine – E B Raley. I came in at midnight and it was pitch black when we got to EB's place. He had stayed with Wilma and me in Scotland about a month previously when we were all complaining of a drought. 'You only think you have a drought,' says EB. 'Wait 'til you see Texas.'

He was right. When I woke up and took a look out the window on that first morning on his ranch, as far as the eye could see there was nothing but brown soil – you'd have thought the whole of Texas had been dug for spuds. Not a blade of grass to be seen. The only green things I could see were prickly pear cactus.

My first judging stint in Texas was in Waco where there was a big rodeo and world championship horse roping being contested. The rodeo started in the evenings with other events held during the day. The sheepdog trial was held in a big indoor arena and it suited me fine, for the weather was very warm and it was nice and cool inside – my first experience of judging a sheepdog trial under cover. It was difficult to get used to judging inside as it was only about a tenth of the size of an outdoor course and so space was cramped. There was not enough scope for a nice wide arc on the outrun, so you had to make allowances for the dogs hitting the walls all the time. And, as the dog couldn't really get far away enough from the sheep at critical moments, they were much more edgy and hard to manage than they would have been on an open course. But all the competitors were in the same boat and we got through it without any complaints.

There were also cattle trials that were interesting to watch. They put the cattle through much the same course as the sheep. A lot of the dogs in the cattle trials were what they call Australian Blue Heelers. They are a small blue low-set dog, not unlike corgies, but a bit larger with stumpy tails. They were quite good at the cattle, but the two border collies that were in the class always managed to beat them.

I really enjoyed the rodeos in the evenings and one night, when the world championship team horse roping was being held, the large coliseum was packed to the rafters – there wasn't an empty seat in it. Apparently it seated about five thousand. After the grand parade the local big-wigs were spotlit and introduced to the crowd. Before I knew it I heard my name being introduced – the expert from Scotland over to judge their sheepdog trials. They must have known which seat I was in because the spot-light came to me and I had to stand up and take a bow. Now that was something new for me.

At the rodeo the most dangerous sport I think I ever witnessed was bull riding. That's a very, very hard way to make a living. Most of the men who do it walk with a limp. The folk that I really admired though, were the clowns. When the bull's rider was bucked off, or if they were lying on the ground and the bull trying to gore them, then the clowns attracted the bull's attention until they got the rider to safety.

I met some very interesting characters at the rodeo. One night at about twelve o'clock when I was in the restaurant

getting a cup of coffee, I was at the same table as two rodeo girls who had been barrel-racing that night. They had been knocked out of the competition and were heading off with their horses to Kentucky for the next competition. They said they would get into Kentucky at about five o'clock the following evening. One of them said she had won about $15,000 that season and she was just breaking even – the other one hadn't won as much as that. They seemed to be on the road all the time. She told me she hadn't seen her kids since February and this was October, but she would soon have to go home and check them out.

Apart from the characters I met, I enjoyed watching the rodeo itself and the entertainment that was laid on. On one occasion two long-horns steers charged into the ring with horns on them like Highland cattle. While they were trotting round the ring a chap picked up a microphone and began to paint us all a picture of what these two steer might be up to.

He says, 'They're crossing the desert and this is their first day.' The steers paid no attention and continued to trot briskly round the ring. But as the commentator counted out day two and day three the steers seemed to move more and more slowly, until they were trudging along step by heavy step, as if it was a real labour just to keep moving forward.

'They haven't had water for three or four days now,' he said, 'and they're getting weaker by the hour.'

At this point they began to stumble and wobble.

'They're about to collapse,' says the commentator. 'They're completely exhausted and dehydrated.'

And then, to the gasps of the crowd, the two steer fell like a stone to the ground. The commentator walked over to where they lay, lifted their heads, pulled a revolver out and fired a shot into each one's forehead. Their heads just dropped.

'Better to put them out of their misery,' he said after he'd done it.

You could have heard a pin drop in that stadium and there with not a movement from those two steer.

After standing looking at them for a good sixty seconds, the commentator gave a whistle and the two steer jumped to their feet and trotted out of the ring.

# Seven Ewe Ranch

After this rodeo, I moved about four hundred miles further south down to Ozona. I then moved on out to Sheffield, which was about thirty miles out of town, west of the Pecos, to stay with Ivan Weir. In the previous year Ivan had moved down from Canada, and was managing a ranch for Bob Childress, the 'Seven Ewe'.

Says he, 'You've never been to Texas until you're west of the Pecos.' So I can now say I've been to Texas.

There is a bridge over the Pecos, but before the bridge there is a place where the old wagons had to be let down on winches to cross the river. You can still see the tracks on the hillside where the old covered wagons were. It's a sort of semi-desert country with about one cow to a hundred acres. There's a big population of Mexican Angora goats on it too.

I stayed with Ivan for a week at the Seven Ewe, a big ranch with a lot horses on it, some cattle, and a lot of goats. It was divided into sections and the whole ranch was watered by deep bore holes and windpumps. You would have seen the Mexican workers head out about the edge of dark to some of the waterholes and they would have lassoed a goat and brought it in and butchered it. That's what they lived on – goat meat mainly.

There were a lot of rattle snakes and Ivan and his wife, Janet, kept a lot of cats. Apparently the cats would kill the small snakes and also act as a sort of snake repellent, as snakes don't like the smell of cats. I watched Janet going across the ranch-yard one day with a cat under each arm. She had a vegetable plot with tomatoes in it and before she went in she sent the two of them into it. Says I, 'Janet, what are you doing that for?' 'Oh, just checking,' she says, 'that there's no snakes in the vegetables before I go in to get some.'

The heat down at the Seven Ewes took a bit of getting used to. One day Ivan said we should head about ninety miles down to Judge Roy Bean's old saloon. It sounded good to me, for with

the heat I was spitting dust and I thought at least there we'll get a cool beer – even a cool coke would have been welcome. We motored down and I needn't say the sun was splitting the trees, for there were no trees. We went down anyway and arrived at Judge Roy Bean's Saloon just on the Rio Grande. I went in and there was an old bottle or two just sitting on the bar with cobwebs on them. There hadn't been liquor sold out of them since 1890. Talk about a let down. It was good to see though. The Old Judge had fancied Lily Langtry and he built a theatre for her. It would only have held about two dozen folk, but if you built a theatre out in that wilderness I would think two dozen would be a good crowd.

## Winter Olympics – Harry Holmes' Ranch

I was to make two more trips to that area in Texas, one of which was to judge the Winter Olympics in January at Harry Holmes's ranch. These are a series of four trials over two weeks.

Harry's ranch was about fourteen or fifteen miles off the highway up a dirt track, crossing creeks on the way. In a motor you couldn't have gone more than five miles an hour or you'd have gone through the roof. The road in was so rough it took a long time to get there, but it was well worth the trip as it was a beautiful ranch and ranch house. But Harry lived there all alone. I said to him, 'Harry, would you not think about getting a woman in here? Do you not feel lonely?'

'Aye,' he says, 'I had a wife a time or two but the last wife I had, she went to the shops one day and never did come back.'

At about six o'clock on those January mornings, the trial organisers had a cook come in on a covered wagon and by about eight o'clock he would have had the breakfast ready. He had his biscuits, or scones as we'd call them, all baked and his cooking done, bacon grilled, all over an open fire. For lunch he would barbecue goat. All very tasty.

There's something different about sitting eating breakfast in the morning, with daylight just breaking and the turkeys gobbling through the country. It put me in mind of the old farms back when I was a boy. Back then each farm reared a few turkeys and you would have heard them gobble. But the wild turkeys seem to live in colonies in Texas and at the break of daylight they make wild gobbling noises. Quite often you would have seen a string of them coming though the trial course if there were no dogs running. They certainly weren't double breasted. They were built for speed. It wouldn't have taken a big oven to hold one. My mother used to say there was a clergyman beside where she was reared who said a turkey was an awkward feed, it was too much for one and not enough for two. Any man if he was hungry could have managed one of those Texas turkeys fine.

# Ozona for the Texas Finals

My last trip out to Texas was to judge the Texas Finals, although they involve more than just Texan competitors. Anybody who has competed in the Texas Trials over the season is eligible to run so you'd get handlers from all over the States. These Texas Finals are run over a week and include Novice, Intermediate and Open classes. Fifty per cent or more of the handlers in the US are lady handlers and the standard of Open work at that trial was very good.

By the time I went out to judge these Texas Finals, Ivan Weir had moved from the Seven Ewe ranch and was working for Gene Perry – a chap who owned a big ranch just on the edge of Ozona. Gene had a lot of oil interests and business in town and bred pedigree Hereford cattle. He also had sheep and goats and Ivan had set up some very good sheepdog trial courses through the ranch. It was an ideal place for the championships.

I met up with a chap Joe Brown while I was in Ozona. Joe had an 18,000 acre ranch about sixty to seventy miles out of town. His wife worked in town and just went home at the weekends. Joe and I motored out one day to the ranch through some very wild country. After about an hour, Joe could see I was feeling the heat so he says, 'There's a fair drive yet to get to the ranch but there's a wee pub where we can have a drink to quench our thirst.' We had to cross a river to get to this place and when we arrived it was no more than a wee tin hut. When we went in there were two old guys in it drinking beer. To get customers in that place you would nearly have to have flown them in by helicopter for I saw no houses near by and we had to motor on nearly twenty miles to get to Joe's ranch.

Joe told me that he couldn't make a living out of his sheep and cattle stock on that 18,000 acres; he also needed the income from the shooting of the deer, quail and wild turkey on the ranch. Apparently the shooting was worth more than all the cattle and sheep ranching put together. He allocated one week to the bow and arrow boys, then let the rifle men in.

Joe had feeders out for the deer. These were driven by car batteries which automatically put food out at regular intervals. Beside these feeders there were hides where the gun-men or hunters would sit. Once the wild deer heard the click of the feeders they came in from all directions. The hunters were allowed to shoot one deer from the hide. They could just take their pick.

Whenever I was out with Joe he shot a rattle snake, threw it in the back of the pickup and took it home to the ranch. A girl who worked on Gene Perry's ranch, where Ivan Weir lived, cooked them and claimed they tasted much the same as chicken. I wouldn't have fancied one.

It was while I was judging the Texas Finals that a chap motored down all the way from Nebraska to visit me. It was a 1,800 round trip from Nebraska to Azona. I had sent him out a dog which he was very well pleased with and he had brought him down for me to see. This chap was big in the Aberdeen Angus world, having sixteen hundred pedigree Aberdeen Angus cows. He sold the bulls in batches of tens and twenties to the ranchers and had a huge petrol motor home that he'd got specially built to go round the sales and the shows. He told me he got six miles to the gallon. When you count that up, six miles to the gallon for eighteen hundred miles, it was a pretty expensive visit but he seemed to be well able to afford it. He must have had a very big ranch for he said he had a cowboy rode the fences most of the time just to check them. They were either very long fences, or it was a very slow horse.

Jim Varnon was a very interesting chap I billeted with when I was in Texas. He lived in Dallas, just on the edge of town. He had business in town, but he was a keen dog handler. He took me one night to the Dallas State Fair – a big show that lasted for three weeks with all sort of sideshows at it. One of the sideshows that caught my eye was with rabbits. You put a coin in and the rabbit drove a steam engine on a wee railway – pulled the cord to hoot the horn and do all these things. There were also ducks that performed in cages behind glass when you put in a coin. But the one that intrigued me most, was a hen that played 'noughts and crosses', or tic-tac-toe as it's called over there. You pressed a button outside and it pressed one inside, and each time it won a game, the hen got a pellet of grain. No matter what I did, I couldn't beat that hen and I watched a lot of other guys and nobody seemed to be able to beat it.

Jim's wife told me a story about Jim and the Dallas authorities when we got back home. Jim was fond of covered wagons, driving at rallies with two mules. He had bought a couple of new mules, and, to get them used to the covered wagon, he took off this day and headed into town. He told his wife it would get them used to traffic. He was a long, long time gone, even for Jim, and there was still no word of him, so she rang up the highway patrol to report Jim and these mules missing. They began to ask a lot of particulars right down to what colour these mules were and a detailed description of her husband.

So she says, 'What are you talking about? Just how many silly buggers would head into Dallas with a pair of mules or how many mule trainers do you think you'll see in Dallas?'

She says, 'If you see a silly bugger with two mules and a covered wagon, that'll be him.'

## All American Championships Oklahoma

The next time I met up with E B Raley was in Oklahoma where I judged the All American Championships over a week, along with Judy Simpson of Scotland and Colin Gordon of Wales.

E B Raley's wife, Francis, was the North American Sheepdog Association Secretary and did everything very efficiently, keeping tabs on me so that I didn't get led astray. But sometimes she had got her work cut out. One day when I wasn't judging, EB took me into Oklahoma City to visit the Cowboy Hall of Fame. This held photographs of a lot of the old famous names of the West such as the top world championship rodeo cowboys and of the old wagons that were used by the pioneers.

All three of us judges at the trial stayed in a wee place called Reno outside Oklahoma City where a bus picked us up every morning before daylight. The bus was driven by a young girl, a school teacher from Alaska, who, as a member of the Association, was helping out with the running of the trial. Most of the winter in Alaska is in darkness. Well she must have thought she was back there, for she picked us up at about half six in the morning and took us to the trial course, where we had to sit nearly an hour in the dark near a cemetery. I couldn't see much sense in it. It was actually an army cemetery, as the trial was being held on what had been a big army cavalry training place which had once had thousands of horses on it. Although it is now an agricultural college, the old billets are still kept as they were. The officers' and cavalry men's billets, and the stabling for the horses, all just as it was one hundred years ago. My imagination could go a bit wild on those dark mornings and I half expected to see a ghost or two coming out of that cemetery. I was always relieved when the camp cook arrived and we could see him get his fire going to start cooking the breakfast. By nine o'clock he would have made a big pot of stew to feed hundreds, stirring it all the time with an enormous spade.

It was my responsibility to judge the All-American Nursery Championships, which were held over two days with over a hundred dogs. Colin and Judy judged the qualifying for the Open Finals while I was judging the Nurseries. Then all three of us judged the Finals on the Sunday over a double-lift course; much the same as our International course, only not so big. The sheep were quite good on the course, but very difficult to shed, for they were used to the coyotes getting in amongst them and so the dog gave them a bit of a fright.

Alasdair MacRae won the Supreme Final and Angie Pickle, a very good handler, probably the best lady handler in the States who could hold her own anyplace in the world, was second. Her husband has a ranch and she is very practical and can read her sheep tremendously well. I was pleased to see that Ivan Weir made the final with Moy, a daughter of the dog, Jim, that he got from me.

## Travels with Marv Brown

As well as the USA, I spent some time in western Canada with Marv Brown, a chap I'd been friendly with over the years. Now Marv was a wheeler-dealer. He promoted events all over western Canada and Montana. I spent a month with him, taking clinics and judging trials from the Swan Hills of Northern Alberta, right down to Saskatoon. We mainly travelled in a motor home. The only time we would have had the luxury of a hotel, was when I was judging or taking a clinic and was put up in the local hotel for my trouble. When you had spent most of the week travelling in a motor home, you were glad to see some home comforts.

The first time I was invited to spend time with Marv, I flew into Saskatoon in Saskatchewan and judged a trial for two days in the big fairgrounds there.

The folk that supplied the sheep were Mennonites whose origins can be traced back to sixteenth-century Europe – Holland, Switzerland, Germany and Prussia – but who fled to North America in the eighteenth century to avoid persecution for their stance on the teachings of the Catholic Church. They felt that the Roman Catholic Church which dictated that everyone in a local community must join its church and pay its taxes, was not focused enough on the needs of the people. The history of the Mennonites is one of wandering from country to country, losing their belongings again and again, and of refusing to defend their lives and possessions through armies and weapons. Whilst they remain a very religious group, they are very modern in their ways.

We were invited to have dinner by the community that had supplied the sheep for the trial, which gave them an opportunity to show us round their farm. The chap explained the different ways of working out there, compared to back at home. He had to bring the sheep into the yard at night, otherwise the coyotes would have killed them out in the fields. It was a very fine place. They were obviously hard-working people and very prosperous, but they also believed in simple living.

Although the Mennonites I met lived a modern life, driving the latest Mercedes cars and working with the very latest farm machinery, Old Mennonites and Amish still farm in the old way, shunning engines and electricity and instead relying on horse power. You can see them travel into town in their bogies, that's a type of wagon, and even the farm equipment is horse-drawn. The men wear long beards and the whole community dresses in an old-fashioned way with hooks and eyes rather than buttons on clothing and bonnets, and long skirts for the women. Everyone speaks highly of them out there as very good farmers. They till the ground and look after their stock perfectly and keep themselves very much to themselves.

I was later invited to stay on a Hutterite colony for a couple of days. The Hutterites are yet another form of religious community hailing from Europe that have settled in North America. The people still speak German among themselves and, unlike the Mennonites, they live in very structured colonies of about forty to fifty families. When the group gets bigger than that, they buy more land and start a new colony. They are apparently expanding very widely in certain areas of Canada. They are prosperous farmers with their own source of cheap labour – each one adopting their own profession within the community. The minister or spiritual leader takes the role of the 'Chief Executive' and is supported by a group of advisers

– the colony manager, farm manager and two or three witness brothers. Together they makes the day to day decisions on behalf of the whole community.

The colony that I spent time with had a large dairy herd, bred a lot of turkeys and kept about four hundred ewes – which was a very large flock of sheep in that area. Whilst they had the best of modern machinery, they lived in fairly basic accommodation. Each family had a sort of wee bungalow where they lived and slept, but where no food was kept or made. There was a communal dining hall, managed by the cooks in the colony and where a bell was rung three times a day to call the community to their meals.

I got friendly with Joe who was the butcher and, during the two days I was there, he was butchering sheep and pigs for the colony for the month. He and his sister lived in a nice tidy wee house together. Her job seemed to be to knit socks for the colony – and perhaps for curious visitors like me. I know I was lucky enough to be given a couple of pairs of socks knitted out of home-spun sheep's wool – made good and thick to keep out the cold there in the winter time. They were so thick I could hardly get them into my boots. In fact, you could have worn them without boots.

I asked Joe if the young ones left the colony when they got up into their teens. He said some of them did, but most of them came back. They couldn't stand the pressure of making a living out in today's world. They don't handle any money in the community. The preacher man does all the buying. They would go into town with him and each one would pick up all that they needed at the shops. The cook decides if he needs anything for the catering and the stock-men if they need anything to look after the stock or machinery or parts. They go and get it, but the preacher man, he does all the paying, which seemed to work fine.

Later in that trip, Marv suggested that we call on a chap who was a rodeo man. We were lucky that he happened to be at home. There was a large sledge at the ranch with a chimney coming up out of it. When I was having a look around this, the chap came over and opened the door and said that his father used to take him and his brothers out to the highway in that old sledge in the winter time to meet the school bus. He said that it was a fair distance out and sometimes, if the bus was held up with the snow, they would have had to sit in it for maybe an hour. There was a wee stove inside and he explained that his father always lit the stove about half an hour before they headed off so it was nice and warm on the cold, cold mornings. When he told me all this I sort of detected in his voice that he was maybe a bit emotional about this sledge and it was unusual to see, given the fairly rough life he seemed to live. Marv was able to explain later that this chap's father had been shot in a range dispute and that he kept the sledge repaired and painted in his memory.

Apart from these diversions, Marv and I travelled around in our motor home, judged trials, and took dog clinics all over the place.

We stopped to take a clinic in a place called Tompkins in Northern Alberta. It was scorching hot and the mosquitoes were bad.

There were about eighteen or twenty dogs in the clinic over two days. Most of them were reasonably good, about three quarters of them were collies, but I had two dogs which were really a problem. One woman had a German Shepherd and the other had a black and tan dog – she said it was an Australian cattle dog, but I reckoned it was a Doberman. The big problem with them was they would do nothing but try to eat the sheep and if I went near them to give them advice they would try to eat me.

Says I to myself, 'What the heck am I going to do with these two boyos?' So I took myself away off for a walk and thought to myself, 'How the heck did I get myself into a fix like this? And more important, how am I going to get myself out of it?'

I sat in the heat and thought for a while and smoked my pipe. As luck would have it, I noticed one of the chaps that I had got to know where I was staying overnight in the local hotel. I called him over and asked him if he could get me a big long stick, something like a fishing rod. So he went away and came back in an hour's time with a big long pole – I think he must've taken it out of his wife's curtains.

We were working in a paddock just beside a covered over sales-yard. A sale only took place there about six times a year, so it wasn't too difficult to get permission to use the sale ring for the clinic. It was too warm for the sheep, so we had to get four or five goats. I put one of the ladies with her troublesome dog into ring with the goats – and the pole. The first lady in had the German Shepherd and I told her to keep the dog behind the goats, although it was clear that all the dog wanted to do was bite the backsides off the poor hot goats. I told her if the dog went to bite the goats, to tap it back with the big long stick

and give it a standard command when she did this. While this spectacle was going on I sat up on the seats outside the ring and drank iced tea and the odd beer. I did the same with the other old lady and her Doberman, or whatever she called it.

I reckoned there were at least two or three things going on: I was cooling myself down drinking iced tea, sitting up in the shade out of the sun, I was keeping the goats from being eaten by the dogs, and I was giving the women good exercise. I'd also like to think that the two troublesome dogs learnt some restraint that afternoon, but I couldn't count on it.

Generally though, most people who attend clinics have a dog with some potential. What I have found over the years is that the benefit they and their dogs get from a clinic is very much in the hands of the handler. A good handler watches and listens. Those who arrive with too many preconceptions as to how to go about things, are unlikely to be the right frame of mind to absorb what is being said and apply it to their own handling. I have had some very good handlers at clinics who would work quietly and diligently on the areas I had spotted that could be improved when working with their dog. Others, less able, but with perhaps too high an opinion of their competence, were less inclined to hear an honest assessment of where improvements were possible. Like in all walks of life, if you're the one who's talking all the time, your brain hasn't got much time for learning.

## Fort Asinabon

From Tompkins I moved on up to Fort Asinabon, right up on the Swan Hills of Northern Alberta, up in grizzly bear country. If you went out for a walk there, signs on the trees warned you to wear a bell in case you came upon a grizzly. Apparently if they heard a bell they moved off from you.

The clinic I took up there was relatively problem-free – all the dogs were border collies. The only problems were the mosquitoes and the heat. I must have drunk gallons of iced tea. Richard Tipton and his wife ran the clinic and the local trial, but it was their boy that seemed to be making a fortune out of the iced tea. He was making gallons of it in the house and going backwards and forwards out to the field where just about everybody was buying a glass. He certainly had an eye for business.

On the Saturday night we went to the Grand Olde Opry which was held in a large village hall in Fort Asinabon. There must have been about three or four hundred folk there. The hall was packed out and the singers were very good – country and western. All the competitors for the trial the next day were at it. There were handlers from right down in the South, Arizona and Texas, who had travelled long distances to be there.

After the first artist performed, the handlers showed their appreciation with a good loud blow on their dog whistles. This had the old folk in the audience shouting and yelling and for a long time nobody was sure why. Eventually there was an announcement from the stage to say that there was to be no more whistling by the shepherds for it was cutting the ears out of the hard of hearing wearing hearing aids. This was the start of what turned out to be a very good trial in Northern Alberta.

The sheep at the trial were supplied by Richard Tipton and were well used to dogs which, coupled with the fact that there were a lot of very good dogs there, made for a trial of a very high standard. A veterinarian from Arizona, Inez Schroeder, had a top class run and won on the first day. The second day was won by Richard Tipton himself which proved very popular, although it was Inez who won over the two day aggregate.

The dog that won the second day's trial for Richard put me in mind of the old dogs years ago that had to work a lot on their own. Richard had to bring the sheep in every night to a pen to keep them safe, not only from the coyotes, but also the cougars or mountain lions in that area. His dog would then have to get the sheep up through the woods back to the fields in the morning, a good half-mile from home, maybe more, leave them there and then come back home. The only thing Richard had to do was let the sheep out the pen and the dog did the rest on its own – a really useful everyday farm dog. This is the sort of dogs we should be trying to develop – dogs that can use their brain.

# The Great Pyreneans

Coyotes were also a problem at Leroy Gatts' place in North Dakota. Over the years I have visited North Dakota, Montana and Wyoming a few times. I know I have found myself in Deadwood City on three occasions, an area I enjoy.

Leroy Gatts was quite a character. He always carried his pliers in his belt. Even when we went to a dinner dance one night and were dressed up, he still had the pliers in his belt. He claimed he had the fastest pliers in the West. That country has miles and miles of barbed wire and I have no doubt pliers are an important implement, but I think he must've *slept* with his pliers.

Leroy's ranch was a sort of mixed farming ranch. He milked dairy cows, had beef cattle and kept a lot of sheep. He also had guard dogs with the sheep – Great Pyreneans – to keep the coyotes off them. They get these dogs bonded with the sheep by rearing them as puppies with a batch of lambs in a pen and feeding them together until they are about six months old. After the dog has spent about six months with the lambs, they take them all out together on to the range to the other sheep and leave the dog and its close friends, the lambs, out there. The dog stays with the sheep and guards them thinking he's one of them. The farmers put hoppers out and only have to go out to feed the animals maybe once a week. It seems to work very well. Apparently years ago in that area, before they got guard dogs, it was nearly impossible to keep sheep. Llamas are also used to guard sheep, but they're not just as good as the dog.

Three cowboys on horseback put out the sheep at the end of the course at this trial, for the dogs to pick up. These cowboys came in the night before with a pick-up truck and a trailer, with three horses in it. They set up camp, lit their camp fire and slept that night under tarpaulins, or tarps as they called them, under the moon. They hobbled the horses so that they wouldn't travel far during the night. By hobbling I mean they strapped their two front legs just a few inches apart and the horses couldn't move very far, but they could still feed and graze through the night. That made them handy to get hold of in the morning.

What I liked about this trial was that Leroy lent me his horse to ride over the range to the trial each morning. It was only a two- or three-mile ride over the range, but about six miles to go round by the road. It was all very efficient – me taking a shortcut and enjoying my ride over in the morning, folk then using the horse during the day for errands or to relay messages while I was busy at the trial, and then me having him to come home on at night. I never thought I'd be riding the range, but there I was.

I took some dog training clinics at Leroy's, one for beginners and one for further advanced dogs. Given the experience of some of the competitors at that trial, there was also a lot of interest in a judging clinic. That involved running three or four dogs which would then be judged independently by the trainees. When it was time to compare notes and check any differences, I had the chance to explain what I believed was important in a trial run, and so why I had or hadn't taken points off.

Ivan Weir, his boss Gene Perry and their wives came up from Texas in two motor homes while I was judging at Leroy Gatts' trial. This was the second trial Ivan had entered that I was judging on this trip and he was having what would probably have been the winning run if he had had the chance to make a good finish. He lost very few or no points until he came to the pen. But just then there was an announcement on the public address system for everyone to call up their dogs and for the competitor to get off the course.

I was fairly bewildered as to what was going on, until I looked up and saw what looked like two Shetland ponies coming over the skyline. It eventually became clear that they weren't ponies. They were the guard dogs, the Great Pyreneans, who had smelt the strange dogs from a distance and were coming over to protect their sheep. The announcement and hurry to gather up the dogs was just in time otherwise the Great Pyreneans would have tried to kill the collies.

Apparently it is always a problem in that area when a handler gets a new sheep dog. The Great Pyreneans can travel long distances to kill a strange dog and so it's really important to allow them to get to know the working dogs. It seems they can't keep these valued guard dogs close to towns or built-up areas as they would kill all the dogs they found.

So on this occasion I had to give Ivan a re-run. Of course his points stood up to the pen, but his next batch of sheep were a bit spooked and he never actually managed to get them in the pen.

It was a bit of a disappointment, as the dog Ivan was running was Jim, a dog he had got off me a couple years previously. Along with Mickey I had won the Brace in the BBC programme, *One Man and His Dog*, in 1988 with him. Knowing the dog very well, I knew he was good at the Pen and the Shed and it was just unlucky that Ivan had to go through a re-run and have an unsettled set of sheep, but it couldn't be helped. That's why they call them trials. Sometimes the sheep win.

Overall, the running at this trial was very difficult. The sheep behaved badly and I suggested to the committee that the course had maybe something to do with it. After the two days trialling and before I left there to move on, the secretary asked me if I would mark out the course for the trial the following year. I was glad to have the chance to change it and put it up to my way of thinking – what I thought would be less difficult for the sheep, especially the weaker sheep. There were some very steep hills, so I set up the course so not all of the sheep had to tackle them. I was asked to come back the following year and judge the trial on the revised course, which I did. The running was much better. Whether it was the sheep, the dogs or the course I can't be sure, but I got the credit for it anyway.

# Budrow & the Buffalo

I moved from Leroy's in North Dakota about a hundred miles farther west and stayed with a chap, Bud Budrow, and his wife. Bud was quite an interesting character too. He had been a professional race jockey for most of his life and was also a fully qualified farrier, looking after the needs of a lot of ranch horses in that area. Since my visit he has gone on to manage the sheep stock for one of the biggest ranching outfits in Texas and Argentina. But at that time Bud had set himself up to train other people's dogs for trialling. He had built himself a lovely ranch house with a lot of very stylish kennels and already had about thirty dogs on his books. He'd be out training at all hours. In fact his whistles woke me one morning at breaking day-light and when I looked out into the paddock, he was working with a young dog. It was just four in the morning.

Bud became one of America's most successful dog trainers. I took him out a puppy, a son of Dick's, when it was only twelve weeks old and was very pleased to see Bud and that same puppy on the USA team at the World Championships at Tullamore in Ireland in 2005. He ran very well despite conditions in Tullamore being different to what he was used to at home, and worked the sheep in much the same way as his father – always on his feet, a good outrunner and always in control of the job.

On this particular trip, Bud suggested I visit a guy about an hour's drive from his ranch that raised buffalo. Apparently there is good demand for buffalo meat now, as it is organic. Bud's wife, Betty, took me to this buffalo ranch where we found an old guy living in a mobile home. He must have been about eighty years of age. He and his son ran a range with about three or four hundred buffalo. His son wasn't at home when we called, but he said he would take me out through the buffalo so I could take a look at them. So, he and I got into his old clapped-out pick up truck and set out through the range. It was the time of year when the buffalo had young calves on them and he had big high fences to keep them in. He told me that in the wintertime they try the fences to the south, as the instinct to migrate is still in them. In the summertime they try the fences to get north. Even after all those generations, the roaming instinct is still in them to follow the grass.

Anyway, we went out in this old clapped-out pick-up away across the range, right in among them. When we seemed to be in the most remote part of the range, we got stuck in a wet spot and couldn't get the truck to move. I didn't dare get out to push for there were big bulls about a ton weight grunting round the pick-up already. They don't make a noise like ordinary cattle, they make more just a grunt, a bit like a pig. Anyway, these big bulls were grunting round and soon the cows started to gather around with their young calves. The old boy began to work at it, but the pick-up's wheels just kept spinning deeper into the mud. Says I to myself, 'This old bugger's going to get us buried in here and we'll never get out of this.' His son was away and he said he wouldn't be back for a couple of days. I could picture myself sitting in there for a couple of days and these buggers

grunting round me. I thought to myself, 'Where's Buffalo Bill when you need him?'

Eventually we got out inch by inch and got away out of it. He told me that the reason they gathered round us was that they sensed there was a stranger about and they were guarding their calves. If we had been there any longer the other bulls and cows would all have circled round. He said the buffalo would even circle round a horse when they were gathering them up to get them into an enclosure. So we were quite lucky to have got out of that, for it was a tricky enough situation for a while.

## Old Timers at Deadwood City

During my stay at Bud's, a party of us went one day into Deadwood City in the Black Hills, about a two or three hour drive from Bud's. They call it a city but it is actually just a country town which is kept in the old style, with the old saloons and the verandas and walkways at the front kept just the same.

We spent quite a while in Number Ten Saloon where Wild Bill was shot. They keep the table where he was shot on display complete with a hand of aces and eights just lying on it – the 'dead man's hand' – allegedly the hand of cards he was playing when Jack McCardless shot him in the back. Jack was arrested across the street in the saloon just opposite.

The chap who was in charge of the gambling in Number Ten, Jim, was a keen dog handler and made us all very welcome.

Number Ten has a lot of famous photographs, including some of Wild Bill and an old guy, Potato Creek Johnny, who apparently found the largest gold nugget in the Black Hills. And then there's Calamity Jane's photograph. She and Wild Bill are both buried in the cemetery in town – Boot Hill as they call it there. Number Ten is very much kept in the old style, with sawdust on the floor and saloon girls, probably working there for the summer, who put on a floor show every few hours. It stays open for twenty-four hours and has plenty of souvenirs for sale – including knickers with Number Ten Saloon on them and garters complete with a gun holster and a wee gun in it. I asked the girl in our company if she would go up and buy me a pair of these knickers and a garter to take home to my wife, Wilma.

She came back down and she says, 'They want to know is it for a man or a woman?'

'Oh,' says I, 'it's for a woman.'

'What size of a woman would that be?'

I wasn't really too intimate in sizes but I held my hands about ten or twelve inches apart. Says I, 'Something like that size.' She gave out a laugh but eventually managed to procure a set for me to take home to Wilma. She might have worn the knickers but I don't think Wilma ever did wear that gun.

The ranches around where Bud lived were very large and quite a few cowboys work on them. During the time I stayed with Bud, the cowboys were running a barn dance or a 'hoe-down' as they call it there, which we were all invited to. Now that was something different. The cowboys dancing in their cowboy boots and their big hats – just like something you would have seen in the John Wayne films, shuffling about in this old barn. It was comical to watch. Although I joined in, I never really got into the right shuffle.

During that evening I met an old guy who was reared on the ranch where the hoe-down was being held and who was just home for a holiday. He told me that when he and his two brothers were boys, there wasn't room for them all in the ranch-house, so they slept in a log cabin. In that part of the country there is snow all winter and it's very, very cold. No matter how well they had the cabin blocked up, when they woke in the morning, a certain amount of fine powder snow always got in and would be on top of the blankets. He told me that when he was getting up in the morning to get dressed and go over to join their father and mother and sisters for breakfast, they had to get out of bed very carefully so as not to disturb the snow. If they were too hasty it would get in under the sheets and melt. Now that's what I call pretty tough rearing.

## Floods in Iowa

We moved on from Bud's via a trial in Wyoming which was held on a polo ground, to Doug Peterson's ranch in Iowa.

Doug's main enterprise on the ranch was pigs. He had hundreds of sows and he took the little piglets off them when they were about two weeks old and put them in special rearing units. It meant that each sow had only a short time to feed and rear her piglets and so could produce more piglets in the year.

Doug held a trial at his ranch, quite a good trial. A few of us arrived in a sort of convoy of motor homes on the run down from Wyoming. A lot of the motoring was on dirt roads through the great plains and some places where the names were quite familiar – Sundance, Powder River and the Great Missouri.

After we crossed the Great Missouri, we called in to see an old chap that had a jack donkey that was fifteen hands high. I didn't know they could grow so big. It's unheard of over here. The largest ever I knew in Britain was 13.2 hands high. But he imported this from Mexico. Mammoth Jacks they called them. He bred mules off this large donkey and had two mules that were 16.2, as big as any large work horse you would see back home. They were bred off a Belgian mare that was 18 hands.

I happened to say to him that mules had a bad reputation for kicking. He says, 'Come here till I show you something,' and he let the two mules out of the paddock and led them into the stable, one in each stand. He put a taste of oats in each pot so they could feed and then called what I took to be his grandchild, a wee girl about eight year old, into the stable. She went in between the front legs of these two big old mules and out behind them while they were feeding. I wouldn't like to see anyone belonging to me doing that when a horse was feeding. But he said the mules were very brainy. He said that if you treat them well, they treat you well in return, but if you treat them badly, they get their own back. And he said that if a mule did kick it never missed.

Judging at Doug Peterson's trial turned into another of these unexpected dramas I seemed to be in the habit of running into. We were judging out of an open cattle trailer set on top of the hill, which had a great view right over the ranch house and all the motor homes set out in a big flat field down at the house. From this vantage point I watched as the skies started to get dark and then got really black. After a very short time folk began running to their motor homes for shelter. Within five minutes there was no one left in the open, except the chap that was competing and the lady beside me who was keeping the scores and doing the time-keeping. Both of us were still in the open trailer when all of a sudden there was a flash of lightening and sparks ricocheting off the bars of the trailer. Says I to the girl, 'I think it's time we weren't here.'

But the rain was hammering down before we could tell the competitor on the field to stop, get our papers and things gathered up and get into the relative safety of the pick-up truck. I had never seen rain like it. After a very short time there was a wall of water coming down the glen to where the motor homes were all parked, washing out the fences and liberating Doug's sows as it came.

There was a scramble to untie dogs from the motor homes otherwise they would have been drowned in the torrent that was now rushing through the field. Feeding utensils, deck chairs and sun umbrellas were being washed down a creek beside where the motor homes were all parked. That creek had been dry until this flash flood appeared. And in amongst it all, were Doug's pigs, squealing and darting around like mad things in the mud.

Once folk had got to grips with the scale of the storm, they soon sprang into action and had tractors towing the motor homes up onto higher ground. I never saw a flood coming up so quick and such a drama ensue, but inside an hour the sun was shining bright again and the flood had gone down. But it took a lot longer to get Doug's stray pigs gathered up and closed in so we could resume the trial.

## The Deadwood Challenge

When I went out to stay with Marv Brown again he had moved down from Manitoba in Canada with his new wife and had bought a huge ranch in Montana. Apparently the chap that built the ranch house built it so grand he went bankrupt and had to sell out.

I stayed there with Marv for about ten days or so before we moved on. While I was there, I ran clinics at his ranch and judged a trial nearby. But you never knew what Marv was up to. He was always planning something.

He told me that there was a challenge trial in Deadwood. It was quite a long drive down to Deadwood, but I always enjoyed those drives through the Black Hills, past Rushmore where the presidents are carved in the hillside on the rocks.

He said nothing about this challenge trial during the trip.

It wasn't until we arrived in Deadwood the night before the event that he began to open up a bit.

'You know,' he says, 'you'll need a wee bit of an insight into this. What I've organised is a challenge between the American handlers versus the Scottish handler, and,' he says, 'you're the Scottish handler. You can run my old bitch.'

She had been coming out with me for a bit of a stroll at the ranch and would do some work for me, but she was a long age and was going blind. I knew her quite well, for a very good friend of mine and one of the nicest handlers you'd ever wish to meet, the late Davy Mateer of Scotland, had run her at the Scottish Nurseries. The day he ran her in the Scottish Finals down at Dumfries, he told me he was sending her out to Marv. But this was a long number of years previous and she was well past her sell-by date by this time.

The trial was to be held in the Fair Ground, a sort of a showground arena just in the town. We had gone down the day before because Marv had to set up the course – and it was more like an obstacle course. There were all sorts of things that were never seen at trials before. It wasn't a big course but the way Marv put it up it was nearly impossible to do.

To make matters worse, Marv had arranged for an old guy to go around with a public address system out of his big van. He seemed to live in that van. He must've had twenty dogs and they were always with him in it. There was a bit of a hum off him. You always wanted to be upwind from him to keep the hum off you, for he slept in the van with those dogs. But he was quite an interesting old boy. He had been in Britain during the war with the Americans and that's where he said he had seen the dogs working in the Border area of Scotland and how he had become so interested in border collies. I don't think he had ever competed, but he had a notion of border collies and did this round of trials with Marv as a hobby.

So he set up in the middle of town and started to fire a revolver into the air to gather the crowd around and to advertise this great challenge match. We then retired into Number Ten where Jim looked after us and entertained us. On the day of the trial we each had to compete in a qualifying round, the best three then going through to the finals.

Marv had gone to the expense of arranging a pipe band which he brought about 300 miles down from Canada to pipe me, the 'Scotchman', into the ring. Mohamed Ali couldn't have made a grander entrance. As it happened the bitch ran quite well, so I did manage to get into the final which was billed for later on that night when there would be bigger crowds in town. The problem was it had to run under floodlights and this bitch that I was running of Marv's had even more trouble seeing in artificial light. When I went out to run under the floodlights she was stone blind. Dogs that have PRA or cataracts can see nothing in bright sunshine or bright lights. I would have needed a crash helmet on her for she was bashing into the obstacles. With a lot of trouble I got the sheep round the course but I was last of the qualifiers in the final.

I remember telling Marv in the Number Ten Saloon later on that night, if he had got me a better dog, I could have managed without the pipe band.

## California Girls

I was invited to judge a trial in California held away up in one of the fruit and cotton growing valleys. Wilma and I flew into Los Angeles and then took a short flight to Bakersfield – one of the bumpiest rides I've ever been on in a small plane in my time. It was worse even than flights in helicopters in the Highlands of Scotland. You would have thought you were sitting on a bucking bronc. We were nearly thrown out of our seats. Thankfully the ride only lasted about thirty minutes and we were close to the end of what had been a very long journey. The last leg was a drive to stay with George Griff, a building contractor who keeps some Barbado sheep and a keen trialist.

George had organised for me to take one or two clinics on the days before the trial started. One old guy came up to me and he says, 'Afore ye start, I don't want to pay fifty dollars to have my dog abused,' he says, 'for I've had him at a few clinics and the ones who took the clinic they were very sore on my dog and I want to get some insight into what way you train before I pay my money.' 'Oh,' says I, 'don't worry. The way I train you could almost do it to music.' So he seemed happy enough – and that's the secret in clinics, keep the folk happy, don't abuse their dogs, explain the good points of the day and quietly explain how to correct their weak points.

At the first trial I judged, well over seventy per cent of the handlers were ladies and the weather being warm, they were fairly well stripped down. There were a lot of competitors and not all were up to the grade so, to keep a bit of pace and interest to the trial, we decided to set a standard that competitors had to achieve in order to be allowed to complete their run. If they lost a critical number of points, they would be eliminated to save time.

Now George was a big man of about twenty stone at that time and had fairly strong views on how things should be done. The trial was nearly finished with the last competitor out on the course. She should have been off maybe half way round the course, as she had lost enough points but, being the last competitor, I let her carry on, for we had to check the prize list and it was going to be about ten or fifteen minutes before we were ready to announce the prizes. George wasn't aware that we were busy and had reason to keep the crowd entertained for a few more minutes. Instead he seemed convinced that maybe we were giving this pretty girl some preferential treatment. I can see him yet marching down the field yelling, 'Get her off! She's bound to be over the limit.' 'Ough George,' says I, encouraging his indignation, 'have a heart. I couldn't chase that off the park.' By his demeanour I think he took me a bit too seriously.

On another day, George took us to see the giant redwoods

in Sequoia National Park – about an hour's drive from his place. Now these are huge trees – the largest of them are about thirty-five foot in diameter and some are a thousand years old. They reckon one of them is the oldest living thing on earth.

We ended up that day on an Indian reservation where the Indians had started a casino. There were hundreds and hundreds of one-arm bandits, gambling tables and restaurants. By the time we got there it was fairly late in the evening but it wasn't long before George claimed to have won three hundred dollars. I don't know whether he did or not. As far as I could see he had lost about five to win the three, but he bought us all a meal anyway. The gambling was open twenty-four hours a day. When we were leaving at about eleven or twelve at night, the bus loads were still coming in. The Indians are on to a winner there all right.

## Pennsylvania & Maryland

For two consecutive years I was invited to judge trials organised by Mary Brigoff in Pennsylvania and Maryland. It was on the way down to the Pennsylvania trial that Mary and I had a very hair-raising experience – and not quite the start to the trip I was expecting.

She had picked me up at the airport in her large motorhome, specially fitted out with four kennels in a section built in a front overhang. To get the dogs up into their own kennels she had a big heavy board which the dogs walked up. Once the dogs were inside their kennels, Mary put this board on the top. That all seemed fine and very organised and was apparently something she had been doing for years.

We'd picked up a fair speed in the outside lane of the freeway when we both had a heavy thump on the head. The plank of wood had slid down and nearly knocked us both out, blocking the view ahead of us out the windscreens and pinning us against our seats. Mary slammed on the brakes and as luck had it at that time of day, there wasn't much traffic on the road. After a while I managed to wriggle free of the board and get it off the top of Mary into the back of the lorry out of the way. Not being one to get too flustered, Mary was soon on her way again. But it didn't end there. As a result of that thump on the head, Mary passed out the following morning and had to spend the following two days in hospital.

Not before she'd got me to the trial in Pennsylvania though, which was run at Walt Jagger and his daughter, Cherie's, place. Talk about a trial course being set up to perfection. The obstacles were all painted white with flowers on each of the panels. I had never seen the breed of sheep they had before – Kataudins they call them – a special breed which you don't have to shear. Some of them are white and some of them have got brown markings on them. Like Barbados they can stand a lot of running and never seem to tire which makes them ideal for dog trials.

The sheep were very good at this trial and there were very, very large entries. If it hadn't been for the quality of the sheep and the first-class organising it would have been impossible to get through them all.

On the Saturday one of the marquees had a board floor and they ran a dance. Walt himself had a dance orchestra in his younger years, but was retired now, being nearly eighty. He played the saxophone the first night of the dancing and was real good.

On the Sunday when the finals were due to take place, the local clergyman held a church service in the same marquee for the competitors and all those living around. The minister asked me if I could contribute to the service. Now that's not really something I'm too experienced at so I declined his invitation.

After Pennsylvania we moved back up to Mary Brigoff's in Maryland for the final trial, on a course just in front of Mary's house. Mary had bought the land with no house or anything on it and had then built a beautiful ranch-house and a barn that was like a palace. There were railings round all the fields and the place was all planted with shrubs – just a real picture post-card setting. She also had Kataudin sheep which worked very well with the dogs and the running were very, very good.

This and Walt's trial were both very enjoyable and I had no difficulty in making my way back the following year to judge them again. The following year Walt had broken his ankle and he competed out of a golf buggy – quite successfully, apart from the Shed.

But the hospitality was tremendous. Walt took me for a drive through the forest and through some dairy farms to see where a tornado had come through a few weeks previously. I wouldn't have liked to have been there then. It had cut a path through the forest about a hundred yards wide, like a giant reaping machine had come through and just cut the trees off two or three feet off the ground. In a small town one half of the houses had been completely demolished. He said a lot of the houses and cars were in the lake and they were going to have to start to clear it out. Meanwhile, the other part of the town was not touched at all.

The Maryland trial, like Walt's in Pennsylvania, was well managed and the running was very good. I had only one complaint. There was a chap that seemed to get on great with me the first day or so. He said he wouldn't buy his dogs from anyplace ,only Ireland, and his dogs were all Irish. I knew what he was up to. He was actually the first man I disqualified for gripping. The result was that as soon as he was off the field he came marching up to the judge's box and he says to me, 'It's impossible for that to be a grip for the tusks have been taken out of that dog. It couldn't possibly have been a grip.' Says I, 'I'm very easy pleased with a grip. It doesn't have to be perfect to satisfy me.' So he turned on his foot and marched away very sharply. When he was twenty yards away he turned and gave me a long stare. I think he thought he had an intimidating look about him but I didn't let it worry me.

Mary's sheep were very well used to dogs. She takes in a lot of students to teach them to handle dogs with the result that her sheep got a lot of work and during the trial there was very, very little wrong with a lot of the top runs. In fact Alasdair MacRae won it on the last day, with maybe as good a run as ever I judged in my life. It was a run that you could have given full points to and nobody could have said there was anything wrong. But just to let him know that I was watching, I did take a couple off. He won though with his dog Nan, the bitch that had won the International in the UK before he had gone to live in America. Since arriving in America he has won the All American and Canadian Championships every year. I think he has won it four or five times in a row. In fact, Ralph Pulfer always said that Alasdair was the biggest robber to hit the USA since Jesse James.

## Dick's Finest Achievement

When I sold Lagnaha we took on Well House Farm on the edge of Kirkcowan village in Wigtownshire. It was a former dairy farm of around 180 acres and was situated in the centre of sheepdog country, six of my close neighbours being Scottish team members. The late Murray McCormick who farmed Wellhouse before I purchased it was a keen dog trialist and team member. J M Wilson's famous Nap was born a short distance away at Maitland Farm. Like most parts of the country, there were characters who could tell good stories.

Newton Stewart Auction Mart was a short distance away. Blackface Rams have been sold there at world record prices, and some of these prices are recorded in the *Guinness Book of Records*. The first time I attended Newton Stewart Ram Sales was in the early 1950s when I purchased a ram lamb for £60. The transaction was recorded in the *Scottish Farmer*. To be mentioned now, the price would be many thousand pounds. The record price at Newton Stewart at that time was £1,300 for a Falbae bred lamb, called Jimmie Craig, which was sire of the £60 lamb that I bought. The record price now for a Blackface Ram is around £80,000.

My last farm in Scotland was in Renfrew outside Paisley. The BBC filmed on that farm when I represented Scotland on the *One Man and his Dog* programme – I'd represented Ireland when living in Millisle and then again when I retired home to Antrim. We had lived on that farm only three years when I was approached by a business man who asked if I would sell it to him. I said I would think about it but he called with me again and we made the deal over a cup of coffee. I would have been keen to buy a farm in Scotland again, in fact an auctioneer friend had one in mind for me, but we decided to take the opportunity to come back to Ireland, as I was due to retire in a few years.

So it was only a matter of time until I came full circle home to Ireland, this time to a hill farm at Mallusk in County Antrim where I keep a few cattle but mainly sheep – a flock of Pedigree Blue Leicesters and Scotch Blackface. The farm is a very pretty but windy spot being high up on the hills which look down over the glens of Antrim and Belfast Lough.

Although mainly retired, I continue to breed sheep and judge trials and over the years I have held many successful sheepdog trials at my farm in Mallusk. Like the seasoned old sheepdog handlers on the Highlands and Islands of Scotland, I'm still looking for that dog with natural talent and style and the ability to think for itself to win the respect of its sheep.

Which brings me to a final story which I think sums up all that is special about the border collie.

Early one morning when going to carry out a routine check of the sheep, I was faced with a heart-wrenching scene. Dick and I walked round the fields and came on dead sheep everywhere. Sheep were stuck all around the hedges where they had been savaged by local domestic dogs during the night and their wool was torn and spread all around. Some of those that were not

*Winner of First Prize Gimmer Supreme Border Leicester Champion and Reserve Interbreed Champion at Royal Ulster Show.*

dead were badly injured and had to be put down. One of these sheep was particularly special. She was born and bred at the farm and had just won First Prize Gimmer (a one-year-old ewe), Supreme Border Leicester Champion and Reserve Interbreed Champion at the previous Royal Ulster Show. To see the state of those sheep would have brought tears from stone.

The surviving sheep were understandably terrified, yet when they saw Dick, they began to creep out from the hedges and their hiding places and one by one gather around him. It was a strange and very moving sight which I will never forget. They had just been savaged by and lost many of their flock to dogs, so to most it would seem almost unbelievable that these same sheep should put their trust in another dog – and so soon.

But that morning they demonstrated the real respect they had for Dick, a vote of confidence for the way he had worked with and protected them over the months and years they had known him. I stood aside and watched as the sheep began to take comfort and become more settled in Dick's presence.

I ran Dick in five Irish Nationals, five times he made the Irish Team, and three times he made the Supreme Championship, but I will always think of this scene with the frightened sheep as his greatest achievement – and a real illustration of why the sheepdog is as important as the handler in working with sheep. It's a partnership, not a master-servant relationship. Remember that and you'll reap the rewards.

# Glossary

**Away to me** – The voice command for sending a dog out to the right.

**Brace** – Working with two dogs.

**Cast Ewe** – Sheep from hill farms are typically sold to lowland farmers as 'Cast Ewes' after they have had four crops of lambs. On better grazing they can then go on to produce another two to three crops of lambs. Cast Ewes must be 'correct', meaning they must have all their teeth and be healthy in all respects.

**Come Bye** – The voice command for sending a dog out to the left.

**Crook** – The shepherd's crook is a long staff often used to catch sheep that need attention. It is traditionally crafted from hazel wood and has a curved horn at the top which can be decorated with carvings and lettering.

**Drive** – Taking the sheep in a straight line away from the handler. In a trial situation this involves taking the sheep around a triangular-shaped course through two sets of gates on the way.

**Exhaust Pen** – The place where the sheep which have just completed a trial run are driven.

**Fetch** – The action, immediately after the Lift, of the dog bringing or driving the sheep towards the shepherd. In a trial environment the sheep must be brought in a straight line between a set of gates. This simulates the real working possibility of a dog having to bring sheep through a number of fields to get them to the handler.

**Flank** – A correcting movement sideways by a dog to keep the sheep from going off course as he drives them forward.

**Gimmer** – A one-year-old ewe.

**Grip** – The movement of a dog to bite the wool or nip the nose of a sheep and one which should only be made on the command of the handler when the dog is facing particularly aggressive sheep. If a dog grips his sheep at a sheepdog trial, it results in disqualification.

**Heavy sheep** – Sheep that are reluctant to move away from the dog.

**Holding Pen** – The pen at the top of a trial field where the sheep are held and then released in groups (usually of four or five) for each run.

**International Sheepdog Society (ISDS)** – Since 1906, the governing body for registered working Border Collies of British stock and the body responsible for the standards and management of the four National and International competitions each year. Its stated aim is to 'stimulate interest in the shepherd and his calling and to secure better management of stock by improving the shepherd's dog'.

**Lift** – The point at which the dog arrives behind his sheep and begins to get them moving forward. At a trial this is immediately after the dog has finished its Outrun.

**Light Sheep** – Sheep that are easy to move off and quick to react to the dog.

**Novice & Open Class** – There are various level of entry to sheepdog trials and the novice class is generally for dogs that have not won a prize in any previous trial. The Open Class is for dogs of any age or track record.

**Nursery Trials** – The aim is to give young inexperienced dogs up to three years old, which have not been placed in any competitions other than Nursery Trials, some exposure to trialling.

**Outrun** – The first part of a trial where the dog leaves the side of the handler – on either the left or the right – at the bottom of the course and runs in a wide arc to arrive just behind the sheep at the top of the course.

**Pen** – Towards the end of the trial course when the dog is required to drive the sheep into a fenced enclosure.

**Power** – When referring to power in a dog, we mean that they have the confidence and character to control and demand respect from the sheep. A good dog only shows the true extent of his power when he needs to.

**Registered dog** – Pedigree Border Collie puppies (from ISDS-registered parents) must be registered with the ISDS before they are six months old. Dogs must be registered with the ISDS to be able to enter National and International competitions.

**Scutching** – The action of beating flax to soften the straw and loosen the waste material before it is sold to the linen mill.

**Shed** – Separating one (a single) or more sheep from the flock.

**Shedding ring** – a marked ring forty yards in diameter where, during a trial, the dog carries out the Shed.

**Tup** – a male sheep or ram.

**Turn-back** – A command to the dog to leave one set of sheep and go back for others that have been left behind.

**Weak dog** – a dog that will back off or turn away from a challenge from a sheep.

Wether Lambs – A castrated male lamb.